D0688759

# Downtown

## Savannah Style

The Association of Junior Leagues International, Inc. is an organization of women committed to promoting voluntarism, developing the potential of women, and to improving the community through the effective action and leadership of trained volunteers. Its purpose is exclusively educational and charitable.

This cookbook is a collection of favorite recipes, which are not necessarily original recipes.

Published by: Junior League of Savannah, Inc.

Copyright© 1996 Junior League of Savannah, Inc.
P.O. Box 1864
Savannah, Georgia 31402
www.jrleaguesav.org

ISBN: 0-9613411-1-4
Library of Congress Catalog Number: 96-77769

Edited, Designed, and Manufactured by:
Favorite Recipes® Press
An imprint of

FRP™

P.O. Box 305142
Nashville, Tennessee 37230
1-800-358-0560

Cover Art, *Afternoon in the Garden*, by Charlotte Haynes Pickering
Illustration Undergraduate Student
The Savannah College of Art and Design

Manufactured in the United States of America
First Printing: 1996   20,000 copies
Second Printing: 2000   10,000 copies

To order additional copies of this book, see the order form in the back of the book.

# Contents

# Foreword

Downtown Savannah Style *is not the first cookbook of the Junior League of Savannah; the original,* Savannah Style, *continues to be a resounding success, with 155,000 books in print and a 1994 Southern Living Hall of Fame Award to its credit. In the summer of 1995, the League explored the possibility of a new cookbook—not intended to replace* Savannah Style, *but, instead, to supplement it. The new cookbook would concentrate on the cuisine, lifestyle, and ambience at the heart of Savannah, one of the most historic and beautiful cities in America.*

*In the months that followed the announcement of* Downtown Savannah Style, *League members contributed over 600 recipes, which were twice-tested, rated, evaluated, discussed, and reevaluated. The 200 that were selected reflect not only delicious cuisine, but also the changing nature of Junior League membership—busy women with volunteer activities, families, and careers to work around, who still care greatly about the art of fine food and the pleasure of entertaining.*

*To illustrate the new book, the League turned to the Savannah College of Art and Design, located in the heart of the city. Art students submitted original work depicting the magnificent details of downtown, the exhibition was juried, and the winners of the illustration art were chosen, along with the color cover. The League's legacy of fundraising, including cookbook sales, comprises nearly a million dollars contributed to the community since the Junior League of Savannah was founded in 1921.* Downtown Savannah Style *will continue this tradition and is a celebration of the art, architecture, lifestyle, and cuisine of this quintessentially Southern city.*

# Acknowledgements

Downtown Savannah Style *has been created from the excellent recipes contributed by the active and sustaining members of the Junior League of Savannah, Inc.*
*The publication of this book would not have been possible without the dedication and support of all those who cooked, tested, evaluated, and proofread many recipes. A big thanks goes to Mildred Derst for launching the project; Nancy Skinner and JoAnn Morrison for organizing the testing process and recipes sent to the printers; Temple Morrow and team for setting up the art competition and juried exhibition and working with the writers of the accompanying text; Diane Long and Martha Nesbit for researching and writing the text; and Margaret Kempf Lange and committee for their marketing efforts.*

*Millie Green*
*Chairman*

# Introduction

Each year, the Savannah area attracts more than 5 million visitors.
They are lured, certainly, by the area's natural beauty—the lush tropical vegetation,
the multitude of majestic oaks dripping moss, the spectacular sunsets, and the waving
marshgrass bordering miles and miles of tidal creeks.

They come, often, to enjoy the water—to laze on the beaches of nearby Tybee Island;
to fish, ski, crab, or shrimp in the Atlantic Ocean or in the plentiful sounds and rivers;
or to observe a busy port at work, where ships from around the world make their silent way
down the Savannah River past River Street, sliding under an impressive 185-foot-high
bridge to unload their cargoes at the Georgia ports, the twelfth-busiest in the nation.

They come, perhaps, because Savannah has a reputation as The Hostess City,
a city that gladly throws out the welcome mat to strangers and celebrates at the
drop of a hat. It's a place where outsiders can experience the Old South—where people on
the street still nod and say hello, where a waitress asks, "How are you?" and waits patiently
for the answer, where lost-looking tourists are never lost for long, sure to be assisted by
a businessman, a mother with children in tow, or a downtown jogger—all willing to
slow their pace long enough to help.

They come, more times than not, to get a glimpse of the South's glorious past—
a peek offered by walking through and experiencing Savannah's downtown Historic
District—a 2.2-square-mile area that is the city's heart and soul. This is not a museum
setting—although there are spectacular ones located here that show what homes,
furnishings, and life were like in the mid-1800s in Savannah's era of cotton prosperity.
Instead, Savannah is a real city, with real people who live, work, play, and entertain
in the more than 2,300 architecturally and historically significant buildings that have
survived since Savannah's earliest beginnings.

While drifting through downtown, visitors can experience the Savannah story:
Through tour guides, they will be introduced to James Edward Oglethorpe, who arrived
aboard the galley Anne with 120-odd settlers from England in February of 1733.
The weary group pitched tents on a bluff beside the Savannah River and went on to
establish Savannah as the first city in the colony of Georgia. Visitors will delight in the
city squares, part of Oglethorpe's original plan for the city, today refurbished,
perfectly landscaped and manicured, each with its own name, own theme, and often a
monument to someone important in Savannah's history. They will hear of the cotton
merchants who built warehouses five stories high along the river, from which they shipped
and stored cotton, warehouses that have been restored and are now home to museums,

gift shops, and restaurants along Savannah's River Street. Cotton made planters and merchants wealthy, and this wealth created a genteel society that appreciated fine architecture, fine furniture, art, and music, and resulted in a number of clubs and organizations whose members enjoyed entertaining in grand style. Visiting a house museum, appointed as it would have been in Savannah's social heyday, one can only imagine the resplendent teas, balls, and dinner parties that are Savannah's legacy.

Savannah has been the inspiration for individuals who have excelled in many areas. John Wesley, the father of Methodism, preached at Christ Church in Savannah. Johnny Mercer, one of America's most beloved lyricists, is buried in beautiful Bonaventure Cemetery. Clarence Thomas, a lawyer who grew up in a small community on Savannah's marshes, was appointed in 1991 to the U.S. Supreme Court. Savannah's history is rich with colorful characters who have made their mark in religion, art, music, law, maritime trade, industry, business, banking, the media, and medicine.

Although Savannahians relish their past, they are certainly not stuck there. Visitors delight in seeing Savannah go about its business—children splashing in the wading pools at Forsyth Park, innovatively clad art students sketching, and executives enjoying brown-bag lunches on park benches in one of the squares. Savannah's city sounds add to the visual tapestry—whether it is the melodies of the Savannah Symphony Orchestra providing a free city concert to thousands listening from picnic blankets in the park, the rhythms of jazz vibrating from City Market, the clip-clopping of horses' hooves on cobblestones, the ringing of church bells from one of the historic churches, or the giggles from girls who have just heard tales of the inimitable Juliette Gordon Low, founder of Girl Scouting in America— at her girlhood home on Oglethorpe Avenue.

This is a Savannah alive and well, thank you—proud of her past, prouder still of a lifestyle that appreciates beauty, culture, good manners, and good taste. So it is that the Junior League of Savannah has set about to publish a cookbook that celebrates those values as related to food. With the legacy of fine dining (both elaborate and casual) in mind, Junior League members set about to compile a collection of recipes that would honor Savannah's culinary traditions but which would use modern ingredients and kitchen methods.

Recipes were chosen, certainly, to reflect Savannah's location on the Georgia coast, where saltwater nurseries nurture a bounty of seafood, such as shrimp, blue crab, oysters, and fish. Along with local specialties, these recipes also reflect the changing membership of the Junior League of Savannah, a membership of busy cooks who have lived in many locations, have been exposed to much fine food, have entertained extensively, and enjoy fresh ingredients prepared with enough of a twist to make them unusual. In the end, the recipes that were chosen were ones that, quite simply, tasted divine.

Downtown Savannah Style is about downtown Savannah, about Savannah style, about good taste and fine art. Enjoy.

Martha Nesbit—August, 1996

# Downtown Appetizers

## Whitaker Lane

One of the elements of downtown Savannah's style that lends the Historic District such an elegant air is the ornamental cast iron and wrought iron that abounds. Notable examples of the art are almost everywhere the eye falls; indeed, like a Southern belle peeking from behind her fan, most of the city's architecture seems to flirt from behind the lacy iron.

Of all the beautiful ironwork, it is the garden gates that seem to be the very symbol of Southern hospitality. When the gate is ajar, the message to passersby is "Welcome! Come in." When the gate is closed, peek through but do not disturb. Legend has it this tradition was born in the Civil War, when plantation gates that had never been closed were shut against the invading army. Some even refused to close, so long had they been ajar, and owners across the South scrambled for long-lost keys to unused locks. After the war, the gates were again opened, though perhaps never with the same sense of carefree welcome that had been exemplified in the antebellum era.

The iron gate illustrated here is one of the many leading to "secret" gardens tucked amid the splendorous architecture of the Historic District.

# Appetizers

Black Bean Salsa  11
Festive Cheese Ball  11
Garlic Brie  12
St. Paddy's Day Dip  12
Goat Cheese Terrine  13
Gougère  14
Savannah Sin  14
Layered Cheese Lotus  15
Stilton and Walnut Torte  16
Blue Crab Spread  16
Courtyard Crab  16
Crab Points  17
Black-Eyed Peas, Chiles and Cheese  17
Shrimp and Artichoke Dip  18
Shrimp Aspic  18
Bacon Breadsticks  19
Bruschetta  19
Cilantro Pesto Toast  20

Herbed Havarti in Pastry  20
Herbed Goat Cheese and Roasted
   Peppers  21
Party Pinwheel Variations  22
Parmesan-Mustard Chicken Wings  23
Grilled Portobello Mushrooms  23
Mushroom Puffs  24
Herbed Oysters  24
Individual Oyster Tarts with Leeks and
   Country Ham  25
Savory Baked Oysters  26
Savory Stuffed Vidalia Onions  26
Roasted Red Peppers and Feta  27
Smoked Salmon Quesadillas  27
Cold Vegetable Terrine with Tomato
   Coulis  28
Watercress, Cream Cheese and Tomato
   Roulade  29

Whitaker Lane  by Steven Alexander
Sequential Art Graduate Student, The Savannah College of Art and Design

# Black Bean Salsa

*Substitute a jar of chopped pimento for the tomatoes, omit the avocado and the salsa can be stored in the refrigerator for several days.*

Combine the black beans, corn, tomatoes, avocado, onion, cilantro, lime juice, olive oil, wine vinegar, salt and pepper in a bowl and mix gently. Chill, covered, until serving time. Garnish with avocado slices and sprigs of fresh cilantro. Serve with tortilla chips. Yield: 6 cups.

2   (15-ounce) cans black beans, rinsed, drained
1   (17-ounce) can white Shoe Peg corn, rinsed, drained
2   large tomatoes, peeled, seeded, chopped
1   large avocado, chopped (optional)
1   purple onion, chopped
1/4   cup chopped fresh cilantro
1/4   cup lime juice
2   tablespoons olive oil
1   tablespoon red wine vinegar
1   teaspoon salt
1/2   teaspoon pepper

# Festive Cheese Ball

*Wrap the cheese balls in waxed paper, place in a sealable plastic bag, and store in the refrigerator for up to three weeks. Roll in chopped nuts just before serving. Serve at room temperature with assorted party crackers.*

Combine the cream cheese, Cheddar cheese, bleu cheese and dates in a bowl and mix well. Divide into 2 equal portions. Shape each portion into a ball. Roll each ball in walnuts or pecans. Yield: 2 cheese balls.

24   ounces cream cheese, softened
4   ounces sharp Cheddar cheese, shredded
4   ounces bleu cheese, crumbled
1   (8-ounce) package chopped dates
     Chopped walnuts or pecans, toasted

# Garlic Brie

1 (2-pound) round Brie cheese
  with rind
10 sun-dried tomatoes in oil,
  minced
5 tablespoons minced chopped
  parsley
5 tablespoons grated Parmesan
  cheese
3 tablespoons coarsely chopped
  pine nuts
2<sup>1</sup>/2 tablespoons sun-dried tomato
  oil
2 tablespoons chopped fresh basil
12 cloves of garlic, crushed

Remove the rind from the top of the Brie cheese. Place the Brie cheese on a large sheet of foil. Combine the sun-dried tomatoes, parsley, Parmesan cheese, pine nuts, sun-dried tomato oil, basil and garlic in a bowl and mix well. Spread over the top of the Brie cheese; seal with the foil to cover. Chill for 30 minutes to overnight. Let stand at room temperature for 30 minutes before serving with assorted party crackers. Yield: 24 servings.

# St. Paddy's Day Dip

8 ounces cream cheese, cubed,
  softened
8 ounces cooked corned beef, finely
  chopped
1 cup drained chopped
  sauerkraut
1 cup shredded Swiss cheese
1/2 cup sour cream
1 tablespoon catsup
2 teaspoons finely chopped onion
2 teaspoons spicy brown mustard

Combine the cream cheese, corned beef, sauerkraut, Swiss cheese, sour cream, catsup, onion and mustard in a bowl and mix well. Spoon into a small baking dish. Bake, covered, at 375 degrees for 30 minutes; remove the cover. Bake for 5 minutes longer or until brown. Serve warm with rye crackers or party rye bread. Yield: 2 cups.

# Goat Cheese Terrine

*The Goat Cheese Terrine will keep for several days in the refrigerator. Exact amounts of cream cheese and goat cheese are not critical. Use more or less depending on your taste.*

Line a 3x9-inch terrine or loaf pan with plastic wrap, leaving enough overhang to cover. Combine the basil, asiago cheese and 2 teaspoons garlic in a food processor container. Process until blended. Add 8 ounces cream cheese, 4 ounces goat cheese, 1/4 teaspoon salt and 1/8 teaspoon pepper. Process until smooth. Spread in the prepared pan. Combine the sun-dried tomatoes and 1 teaspoon garlic in a food processor container. Process until chopped. Add 8 ounces cream cheese, 4 ounces goat cheese, 1/4 teaspoon salt and 1/8 teaspoon pepper. Process until blended. Spread over the prepared layer; seal with the plastic wrap. Chill for several hours to overnight. Uncover and invert onto a serving platter, removing the plastic wrap. Serve at room temperature with bland crackers, toast points, sliced French bread or pita chips.
Yield: 10 to 12 servings.

| | |
|---|---|
| 2 | cups packed basil leaves |
| 1/4 | cup grated asiago cheese |
| 2 | teaspoons chopped garlic |
| 8 | ounces cream cheese, softened |
| 4 | ounces mild goat cheese, softened |
| 1/4 | teaspoon salt |
| 1/8 | teaspoon pepper |
| 1 | (4-ounce) jar sun-dried tomatoes in oil, drained |
| 1 | teaspoon chopped garlic |
| 8 | ounces cream cheese, softened |
| 4 | ounces mild goat cheese, softened |
| 1/4 | teaspoon salt |
| 1/8 | teaspoon pepper |

# Gougère

| | |
|---|---|
| 1 | cup milk |
| 1/2 | cup unsalted butter |
| 1 | teaspoon salt |
| 1 | cup sifted unbleached flour |
| 4 | eggs |
| 1 1/2 | cups grated imported Parmesan cheese |
| 1 | egg |
| 1/2 | cup grated imported Parmesan cheese (optional) |

Preheat the oven to 375 degrees. Combine the milk, butter and salt in a saucepan. Bring to a boil. Remove from heat. Whisk in the flour until blended. Cook over medium heat for 5 minutes or until thickened and the batter pulls from the side and bottom of the saucepan, stirring constantly. Remove from heat. Beat in 4 eggs 1 at a time. Stir in 1 1/2 cups cheese. Drop by tablespoonfuls 1 inch apart onto a buttered baking sheet. Beat the remaining egg in a small bowl. Brush the tops of the puffs with the egg. Sprinkle with 1/2 cup cheese. Place the baking sheet on the center oven rack. Reduce the oven temperature to 350 degrees. Bake for 15 to 20 minutes or until puffed and brown. Serve immediately. Traditionally baked in a ring shape, it is easier to handle at cocktail time if formed into puffs. May double the recipe to increase the yield. May substitute a mixture of 3/4 cup grated Parmesan cheese and 3/4 cup grated Gruyère cheese for 1 1/2 cups grated Parmesan cheese. Yield: 20 puffs.

# Savannah Sin

| | |
|---|---|
| 2 | cups shredded Cheddar cheese |
| 8 | ounces cream cheese, softened |
| 1 1/2 | cups sour cream |
| 1/2 | cup chopped cooked ham |
| 1/3 | cup chopped green onions |
| 1/3 | cup chopped green chiles (optional) |
| 1/8 | teaspoon Worcestershire sauce |
| 1 | (1-pound) round loaf French bread |

Combine the Cheddar cheese, cream cheese, sour cream, ham, green onions, green chiles and Worcestershire sauce in a bowl and mix well. Cut a thin slice from the top of the bread loaf; reserve. Remove the center carefully, leaving a shell. Cut the bread from the center into 1-inch cubes. Fill the bread shell with the dip; top with the reserved top. Wrap in foil. Bake at 350 degrees for 1 hour. Serve with the bread cubes, crackers or chips. Yield: 20 servings.

# Layered Cheese Lotus

Line a medium bowl with plastic wrap, leaving enough overhang to cover. Reserve 3 slices of the provolone cheese. Line the remaining provolone cheese over the bottom and up the side of the bowl, overlapping the slices. *For the cream cheese layer,* process the cream cheese, pistachios and 1 clove of garlic in a food processor until blended. *For the pesto layer,* process the basil, parsley leaves, pine nuts and 1 clove of garlic in a food processor until blended. Dissolve the salt and pepper in the olive oil and mix well. Add to the basil mixture in a fine stream, processing constantly until blended. *For the tomato layer,* drain the sun-dried tomatoes, reserving the oil. Process the sun-dried tomatoes with a small amount of the reserved oil in a food processor until puréed. *Spread* some of the cream cheese mixture over the cheese slices lining the bowl. Layer the pesto mixture, 1/2 of the remaining cream cheese mixture, sun-dried tomato mixture and remaining cream cheese mixture in the prepared bowl. Cover with the remaining provolone cheese. Bring the edges of the plastic wrap together and secure with a twist tie. Freeze until firm. Remove the plastic wrap. Invert onto a serving platter. Serve with assorted party crackers. May store in the freezer for up to 3 months, removing from the bowl when firm. May reconstitute sun-dried tomatoes and substitute for the sun-dried tomatoes in oil. To reconstitute, place the dried tomatoes with a small amount of water and olive oil in a saucepan and cook for 3 minutes. Yield: 15 to 20 servings.

| | |
|---|---|
| 1 | package sliced provolone cheese, divided |
| 16 | ounces cream cheese, softened |
| 20 | pistachios, shelled |
| 1 | clove of garlic (optional) |
| 1/2 | cup fresh basil leaves |
| 1/2 | cup fresh parsley leaves |
| 1/2 | cup pine nuts |
| 1 | clove of garlic |
| 1/4 | teaspoon salt |
| 1/4 | teaspoon freshly ground pepper |
| 2 | tablespoons extra-virgin olive oil |
| 3 | ounces sun-dried tomatoes in oil |

# Stilton and Walnut Torte

16  ounces cream cheese, softened
1   cup unsalted butter, softened
1/4  cup port
5 1/3  ounces Stilton cheese, crumbled
1/2  cup chopped walnuts

Line a loaf pan with plastic wrap. Process the cream cheese and butter in a food processor until fluffy. Add the wine. Process until blended. Spread 1 1/2 cups of the cream cheese mixture in the prepared pan. Press in 1/2 of the Stilton cheese and 1/2 of the walnuts lightly. Spread with 1 1/2 cups of the remaining cream cheese mixture. Sprinkle with the remaining Stilton cheese and walnuts, pressing lightly. Top with the remaining cream cheese mixture. Chill, covered, until firm. Invert onto a serving platter. Let stand at room temperature for 30 minutes. Serve with assorted party crackers. Yield: 12 to 16 servings.

# Blue Crab Spread

1   pound fresh lump blue
    crab meat
1   small can water chestnuts,
    drained, finely chopped
1/2  cup mayonnaise
3   tablespoons chopped fresh chives
2   teaspoons soy sauce
    Dash of cayenne

Combine the crab meat, water chestnuts, mayonnaise, chives, soy sauce and cayenne in a bowl and mix well. Chill, covered, for 2 hours. Serve with melba toast rounds or spoon into individual tart shells. Yield: 10 to 12 servings.

# Courtyard Crab

1   pound fresh claw crab meat
8   ounces cream cheese, softened
2   tablespoons Worcestershire sauce
1   tablespoon curry powder
2   teaspoons lemon juice
1/2  teaspoon Tabasco sauce
1   tablespoon paprika

Combine the crab meat and cream cheese in a bowl and mix well. Stir in the Worcestershire sauce, curry powder, lemon juice and Tabasco sauce. Spoon into an 8- or 9-inch round baking dish. Sprinkle with the paprika. Bake at 425 degrees for 20 minutes or until bubbly. Serve with your favorite crackers. Yield: 8 to 10 servings.

# Crab Points

Combine the crab meat, mayonnaise, cheese, onion, lemon juice and pepper in a bowl and mix well. Spread evenly over the cut side of muffins. Arrange on a baking sheet. Freeze for 20 minutes or until firm. Cut each muffin half into 6 wedges. Bake at 350 degrees for 20 minutes or until the edges turn brown. Yield: 72 servings.

16 ounces white crab meat
1 cup mayonnaise
1 cup shredded sharp Cheddar cheese
1/2 cup chopped onion
Juice of 1 lemon
Freshly ground pepper to taste
6 English muffins, cut into halves

# Black-Eyed Peas, Chiles and Cheese

Heat the black-eyed peas in a saucepan until hot; drain. Mash the peas with the back of a spoon. Stir in the onion, green chiles, chile liquid and seasoned salt. Fold in the Cheddar cheese, butter and deviled ham. Spoon into a 9-inch round baking dish. Sprinkle with the mozzarella cheese. Bake at 350 degrees for 20 minutes or until bubbly. Serve warm with baked tortilla chips or your favorite crackers. Yield: 8 to 10 servings.

1 (15-ounce) can black-eyed peas
3 tablespoons minced onion
2 tablespoons chopped green chiles
1 tablespoon green chile liquid
1 teaspoon seasoned salt
1 1/2 cups shredded sharp Cheddar cheese
1/4 cup butter, chopped
1 (3-ounce) can deviled ham
6 ounces mozzarella cheese, shredded

# Shrimp and Artichoke Dip

1　pound shrimp, cooked, peeled, chopped
1　(14-ounce) can artichoke heart quarters, drained
1　cup mayonnaise
1　cup grated Parmesan cheese
1/4　cup bread crumbs
2　teaspoons minced garlic
　　Lemon juice to taste

*Shrimp adds a new flavor to an old standby.*

Combine the shrimp, artichokes, mayonnaise, cheese, bread crumbs, garlic and lemon juice in a bowl and mix well. Spoon into a deep baking dish. Bake at 350 degrees for 20 to 30 minutes or until brown around the edges and bubbly. Serve with wheat crackers. Yield: 8 to 10 servings.

# Shrimp Aspic

1 1/2　tablespoons unflavored gelatin
1/2　cup cold water
1　(10-ounce) can tomato soup
8　ounces cream cheese
1　pound shrimp, cooked, peeled, deveined
1/2　cup mayonnaise
1/2　cup chopped green bell pepper
1/2　cup chopped onion
1/2　cup chopped celery

Soften the gelatin in the cold water and mix well. Bring the undiluted soup to a boil in a saucepan. Remove from heat. Add the cream cheese, stirring until blended. Stir in the gelatin. Let stand until cool. Add the shrimp, mayonnaise, green pepper, onion and celery and mix well. Spoon into a 4-cup ring mold. Chill until set. Invert onto a serving platter. Serve with assorted party crackers. Yield: 10 to 12 servings.

# Bacon Breadsticks

Wrap the bacon around the breadsticks. Roll in the Parmesan cheese. Arrange in a microwave-safe dish. Microwave for 4$^1$/2 to 5 minutes. Remove to a wire rack to cool. Store, uncovered, in a container. Yield: variable.

*Bacon slices*
*Traditional breadsticks*
*Freshly grated Parmesan cheese*

# Bruschetta

Arrange the bread slices on a baking sheet. Broil until light brown on both sides, turning once. Rub 1 side of the bread slices with the garlic. Drizzle with the olive oil. Top with the tomato slices; sprinkle with the pepper. Broil for 1 minute or until the olive oil sizzles. Garnish with sprigs of fresh parsley. Serve immediately. Yield: 8 servings.

8    *(1/2-inch-thick) slices French or*
     *Italian bread*
2    *cloves of garlic, cut into halves*
1/4  *cup extra-virgin olive oil*
2    *medium tomatoes, thinly sliced*
1/2  *teaspoon pepper*

# Cilantro Pesto Toast

2 cups (8 ounces) fresh cilantro
1/2 cup fresh parsley
1/2 cup grated Parmesan cheese
1/3 cup pumpkin seeds or pine nuts
1/4 cup extra-virgin olive oil
1 large clove of garlic
1 tablespoon fresh lime juice or lemon juice
1/2 teaspoon salt
1/4 teaspoon freshly ground pepper
1/4 cup mayonnaise
30 baguette slices

*This is an excellent tidbit served either hot or at room temperature. The pesto may be prepared in advance and stored in the refrigerator for up to 2 days.*

Combine the cilantro, parsley, cheese, pumpkin seeds, olive oil, garlic, lime juice, salt and pepper in a food processor container. Process until of the consistency of a coarse paste. Add the mayonnaise. Process until blended. Arrange the baguette slices on a baking sheet. Toast at 350 degrees for 5 minutes or until light brown on 1 side. Cool slightly. Spread the untoasted side of the bread slices with 1 scant tablespoon of the pesto. Bake for 8 to 10 minutes or until hot and bubbly. Serve hot or at room temperature. Yield: 30 servings.

# Herbed Havarti in Pastry

1 sheet frozen puff pastry
1 teaspoon Dijon mustard
1 (12-ounce) loaf Havarti cheese
1 teaspoon dried parsley flakes
1/2 teaspoon dried chives
1/4 teaspoon dried dillweed
1/4 teaspoon dried basil
1/4 teaspoon dried fennel
1 egg, beaten

*This recipe is wonderfully delicious and convenient, as all the ingredients can be on hand all the time . . . so unexpected guests are not unexpected!*

Thaw 1 sheet of frozen puff pastry. Spread the Dijon mustard over the top of the cheese. Sprinkle with the parsley flakes, chives, dillweed, basil and fennel. Place the cheese mustard side down in the center of the pastry. Wrap the pastry around the cheese. Trim the excess pastry; seal the seams. Brush with some of the beaten egg. Place seam side down on a baking sheet. Chill for 30 minutes. Bake at 375 degrees for 20 minutes; brush with the remaining egg. Bake for 10 minutes longer. Let stand until cooled to room temperature. Arrange on a serving platter. Serve with sliced fresh apples, pears or your favorite fruit. Yield: 15 servings.

# Herbed Goat Cheese and Roasted Peppers

*Makes colorful pinwheels.*

Arrange the red peppers on a baking sheet. Roast in a 400-degree oven or broil until the skin is blistered and charred on all sides, turning occasionally. Place the red peppers in a food storage bag and seal tightly. Cool for 10 minutes. Remove and discard the skins. Cut the red peppers into halves; discard the stems, seeds and ribs. Combine the goat cheese, chives, parsley, basil, thyme, garlic, lemon zest, black pepper and cayenne in a bowl and mix well. May add a small amount of whipping cream for desired consistency. Spread over the red pepper halves; roll lengthwise to enclose the filling. Arrange in a dish. Chill until firm. Cut each red pepper roll crosswise into 6 rounds just before serving. Arrange the red pepper rounds on a serving platter. Garnish with sprigs of fresh thyme. Yield: 72 appetizers.

6    large red bell peppers
1¼  pounds (4 cups) mild goat cheese, crumbled
¼    cup chopped fresh chives
¼    cup chopped fresh parsley
3    tablespoons chopped fresh basil
2    teaspoons chopped fresh thyme
2    cloves of garlic, minced
     Grated zest of 1 lemon
½    teaspoon freshly ground black pepper
     Pinch of cayenne
1    tablespoon whipping cream (optional)
     Fresh thyme sprigs (optional)

# Party Pinwheel Variations

### Veggie Variation
| | |
|---|---|
| 8 | ounces cream cheese, softened |
| 1 | envelope ranch salad dressing mix |
| 2 | green onions, minced |
| 4 | burrito-size flour tortillas |
| 1/2 | cup chopped red bell pepper |
| 1/2 | cup chopped celery |
| 1 | can sliced black olives, drained |

### Mexican Variation
| | |
|---|---|
| 8 | ounces cream cheese, softened |
| 1 | (10-ounce) can tomatoes with green chiles, drained |
| 1 | small can black olives, drained, sliced |
| 4 | to 6 ounces ham, finely chopped |
| 1/2 | cup sour cream |
| 1 | small onion, chopped |
| 1/2 | envelope taco seasoning mix |
| 5 | burrito-size flour tortillas |

### Roast Beef Variation
| | |
|---|---|
| 8 | ounces cream cheese, softened |
| 2 | teaspoons prepared horseradish |
| 1 1/2 | teaspoons spicy hot prepared mustard |
| 4 | burrito-size flour tortillas |
| 1 | pound roast beef, thinly sliced |
| 2 | medium tomatoes, thinly sliced, drained on paper towels |
| 1 | medium Vidalia or purple onion, thinly sliced |

*These appetizers must be prepared in advance. Double the recipe for large crowds.*

Mix the cream cheese, salad dressing mix and green onions in a bowl. Spread the cream cheese mixture thinly to the edge of each tortilla. Sprinkle with the red pepper, celery and black olives; roll tightly to enclose the filling. Wrap tightly in waxed paper. Chill for 8 hours or longer. Cut into 1-inch slices. Yield: 40 to 50 pinwheels.

Combine the cream cheese, tomatoes with green chiles, black olives, ham, sour cream, onion and taco seasoning mix in a bowl and mix well. Spread thinly to the edge of each tortilla. Roll to enclose the filling. Wrap tightly in waxed paper. Chill for 8 hours or longer. Cut into 1-inch slices. Serve with salsa. Yield: 50 to 60 pinwheels.

Combine the cream cheese, horseradish and prepared mustard in a bowl and mix well. Spread thinly to the edge of each tortilla. Layer the roast beef, tomatoes and onion over the cream cheese mixture. Roll to enclose the filling. Wrap tightly in waxed paper. Chill for 8 hours or longer. Cut into 1-inch slices. Yield: 40 to 50 pinwheels.

# Parmesan-Mustard Chicken Wings

*These are great to take along to the Savannah Symphony's "Picnic in the Park."*

Rinse the chicken and pat dry. Disjoint the chicken wings, discarding the tips. Sprinkle with salt and pepper. Combine the butter, Dijon mustard and cayenne in a shallow dish and mix well. Combine the bread crumbs, cheese and cumin in a separate shallow dish and mix well. Dip each drumette in the butter mixture; coat with the bread crumb mixture. Arrange on a baking sheet sprayed with nonstick cooking spray. Place the baking sheet on the lower oven rack. Bake at 425 degrees for 30 to 40 minutes or until brown and cooked through. Yield: 6 servings.

| | |
|---|---|
| 20 | chicken wings |
| | Salt and pepper to taste |
| 1/2 | cup melted butter |
| 2 | tablespoons Dijon mustard |
| 1/8 | teaspoon cayenne |
| 1 | cup dry bread crumbs |
| 1/2 | cup grated Parmesan cheese |
| 1 | teaspoon cumin |

# Grilled Portobello Mushrooms

*This recipe was contributed by the Il Pasticcio.*

Combine the thyme, oregano, olive oil, garlic, salt, black pepper and chile pepper in a bowl and mix well. Fill each mushroom cap with 1/4 of the mixture. Place the filled mushrooms round side down on the grill rack; close the lid. Grill for 5 minutes. Turn the mushrooms. Grill for 5 minutes longer. Cut into slices. Arrange on a serving platter. Serve as an appetizer or as a side dish. Yield: 8 to 12 servings.

| | |
|---|---|
| 1/2 | bunch thyme, stems removed, chopped |
| 1/2 | bunch oregano, stems removed, chopped |
| 1/2 | cup olive oil |
| 2 | tablespoons minced garlic |
| 1 | tablespoon salt |
| 1 | tablespoon black pepper |
| 1 | tablespoon red chile pepper |
| 4 | large portobello mushroom caps |

# Mushroom Puffs

2    large loaves sandwich bread,
     crusts trimmed
1    pound fresh mushrooms,
     chopped
1/2  cup butter
6    tablespoons flour
1/2  teaspoon salt
1/2  teaspoon MSG
2    cups half-and-half
1 1/2 tablespoons minced fresh chives
2    teaspoons lemon juice

*Delicious appetizer to freeze and have on hand for unexpected company! Especially good in the winter.*

Roll the bread slices very thin. Sauté the mushrooms in the butter in a skillet for 5 minutes. Stir in the flour, salt and MSG. Add the half-and-half. Simmer until thickened, stirring constantly. Stir in the chives and lemon juice. Spread the mushroom mixture over the bread slices; roll to enclose the filling. At this point they may be packed and frozen for future use. Thaw for 30 minutes before cutting each roll-up into halves, then bake. Otherwise, cut each roll into halves and arrange on a baking sheet. Toast at 400 degrees for 20 minutes or until light brown on all sides, turning occasionally.
Yield: about 80 puffs.

# Herbed Oysters

2    shallots, minced
1    rib celery, minced
2    to 3 tablespoons butter
     Pinch of cayenne
1 1/2 cups cream
1/4  cup white wine
1 1/2 tablespoons minced fresh thyme
1    tablespoon minced fresh parsley
1/2  teaspoon Tabasco sauce
48   oysters
     Salt and pepper to taste
     Toast points

Sauté the shallots and celery in the butter in a saucepan for 1 minute. Add the cayenne. Sauté for 1 minute longer. Stir in the cream, white wine, thyme, parsley and Tabasco sauce. Cook until slightly thickened, stirring frequently. Add the oysters and mix well. Simmer for 2 minutes or until the edges of the oysters curl, stirring frequently. Season with salt and pepper. Serve over toast points. Yield: 4 to 6 servings.

# Individual Oyster Tarts with Leeks and Country Ham

*This recipe was contributed by Elizabeth's on 37th.*

Combine ³/₄ cup flour, ¹/₄ cup butter and cornmeal in a food processor container. Process until crumbly. Add the water in a fine stream, processing constantly until the dough forms a ball. Shape into 1 to 2 circles. Chill, wrapped in plastic wrap, for 1 hour. Shape the dough into 6 circles. Place the pastry circles over 6 individual oiled ovenproof custard cups or over 6 crumpled pieces of foil to form pastry cups. Place on a baking sheet. Prick the pastry with a fork 8 times. Bake at 425 degrees for 10 minutes or until crisp. Carefully remove the pastry shells to a wire rack to cool. *For the filling*, heat 2 tablespoons butter in a large skillet over high heat until melted. Add the country ham. Sauté until brown. Stir in the sherry. Cook until reduced, stirring constantly. Add 2 tablespoons flour. Cook for 1 minute, whisking constantly; reduce heat. Add the whipping cream and thyme and mix well. Simmer until thickened, whisking constantly. May prepare the sauce to this point, cool, then store in the refrigerator until just before serving; reheat before adding remaining ingredients. Stir in the oysters and leeks. Simmer until the edges of the oysters curl, stirring frequently. Spoon into the pastry cups on individual plates; sprinkle with the tarragon. Yield: 6 servings.

## Cornmeal Crust

³/₄ cup unbleached flour
¹/₄ cup butter, chilled, cubed
1¹/₂ teaspoons cornmeal
2²/₃ tablespoons very cold water

## Oyster Filling

2 tablespoons butter
1 cup (4 ounces) minced country ham or prosciutto
¹/₄ cup dry sherry
2 tablespoons flour
1 cup whipping cream
1 tablespoon minced fresh thyme or parsley
2 pints small oysters, drained
2 cups sliced quartered leeks

1 tablespoon minced fresh tarragon

# Savory Baked Oysters

1/2   cup butter
1   bunch green onions, chopped
3   tablespoons chopped fresh parsley
3   cloves of garlic, chopped
   Pinch of rosemary
36   oysters, drained
1/4   cup oyster liquor, strained
1/4   cup Italian-seasoned bread crumbs
1/4   cup dry white wine
2   tablespoons Worcestershire sauce

Heat the butter in a skillet until melted. Add the green onions, parsley, garlic and rosemary. Sauté for 10 minutes. Stir in the oysters and oyster liquor. Cook for 2 minutes, stirring frequently. Stir in the bread crumbs, white wine and Worcestershire sauce. Spoon into 4 ramekins. Bake at 350 degrees for 10 minutes. May also be served hot from a chafing dish and served with toast points. May prepare 1 day in advance. Yield: 4 servings.

# Savory Stuffed Vidalia Onions

4   medium Vidalia onions, peeled
4   ounces cream cheese, softened
3   slices crisp-fried bacon, crumbled
1/4   cup chopped fresh chives
1/4   cup sliced fresh mushrooms
1/4   cup whipping cream
1/4   cup shredded Cheddar cheese
1/2   teaspoon salt
1/2   teaspoon garlic salt
1/4   teaspoon pepper
2   drops of red pepper sauce
20   shrimp, cooked, peeled
   Chopped fresh parsley

Wrap each onion in a damp paper towel. Microwave on High for 10 minutes or until tender. Remove inside pulp carefully, leaving 3 layers of onion. Discard pulp or reserve for another purpose. Arrange the onion shells in a microwave-safe dish. Combine the cream cheese, bacon, chives, mushrooms, whipping cream, Cheddar cheese, salt, garlic salt, pepper and red pepper sauce in a bowl and mix well. Spoon into the 4 onion shells. Microwave on High for 2 to 3 minutes or until heated through. Arrange the onions on a serving platter. Top each onion with 5 shrimp; sprinkle with parsley. Yield: 4 servings.

# Roasted Red Peppers and Feta

*Arrange on a silver tray and garnish with red peppers for a pretty presentation.*

Place the red peppers skin side up on a baking sheet. Broil until the skin is blistered and charred on all sides, turning frequently. Place the red peppers in a sealable plastic bag; seal tightly. Steam in the bag for 15 minutes. Rinse the red peppers under running cold water; remove the skins. Cut into thin strips. Combine the red pepper strips, olive oil and garlic feta cheese in a sealable plastic bag. Marinate in the refrigerator, turning occasionally. Top each bread slice with enough red pepper strips to cover; sprinkle with garlic feta cheese. Broil for 5 minutes or until bubbly; do not burn. Garnish with fresh basil leaves. Yield: 10 to 12 servings.

2   red bell peppers, cut into halves lengthwise, seeded
    Olive oil
    Garlic feta cheese
1   loaf French bread, cut into
    3/4-inch slices
    Fresh basil leaves (optional)

# Smoked Salmon Quesadillas

Combine the goat cheese, horseradish, sour cream, 1 teaspoon dillweed, salt and white pepper in a bowl and mix well. Heat the olive oil in a skillet over medium-high heat for 1 minute. Fry the tortillas 1 at a time in the hot olive oil for 2 minutes or until light brown; drain on paper towels. Spread 2 heaping tablespoons of the horseradish mixture on each tortilla. Arrange the smoked salmon over the tops; sprinkle with 1 tablespoon dillweed. Drizzle with the lemon juice. Cut each tortilla into 6 wedges. Serve immediately. Yield: 18 servings.

2   ounces mild goat cheese
1   tablespoon grated fresh horseradish or drained prepared horseradish
1   tablespoon sour cream
1   tablespoon plus 1 teaspoon chopped fresh dillweed, divided
    Salt to taste (optional)
    White pepper to taste
3   tablespoons extra-virgin olive oil
3   (7-inch) flour tortillas
6   thin slices (4 ounces) smoked salmon
1   tablespoon fresh lemon juice

# Cold Vegetable Terrine with Tomato Coulis

1   tablespoon unflavored gelatin
    Cold water
1   pound leeks, white part only,
    chopped
    Salt to taste
1   pound carrots, sliced lengthwise
8   ounces green beans
2   red bell peppers, peeled, cut into
    strips
12  ounces small mushrooms, sliced
2   tablespoons butter
    Pepper to taste
2¹/₂ cups grated Gruyère or
    shredded Swiss cheese
3   cups whipping cream
9   egg yolks
¹/₂  teaspoon grated nutmeg
    Tomato Coulis (page 29)

*This recipe, beautiful and delicious, originated from the LaVarenne cooking school in Paris, France.*

Soften the gelatin in cold water in a small bowl and mix well. Combine the leeks and salt with enough water to cover in a saucepan. Cook for 8 to 10 minutes or until tender. Drain and pat dry. Cook the carrots, green beans and red peppers in separate batches in boiling salted water in a saucepan for 3 to 5 minutes or until tender. Drain and pat dry. Sauté the mushrooms in the butter in a skillet for 2 to 3 minutes or until the moisture evaporates. Season with salt and pepper. Drain and pat dry. Butter a terrine. Layer the red peppers, leeks, carrots, green beans and mushrooms in the mold, sprinkling the cheese between each layer; do not pack. Whisk the whipping cream, egg yolks, nutmeg, salt and pepper in a bowl until blended. Heat the gelatin mixture in a saucepan until the gelatin dissolves, stirring constantly. Stir into the cream mixture. Pour over the vegetables, making sure the mixture seeps between the layers; cover. Set the terrine in a larger pan; fill the larger pan with water. Bring the water to a simmer. Bake at 325 degrees for 1³/₄ to 2 hours or until the side is set, but the center is still soft. Let stand until cool. Chill for 4 hours or up to 1 day before serving. Unmold onto a serving platter. Cut into ¹/₂-inch slices. Serve with Tomato Coulis.
Yield: 10 to 12 servings.

# Tomato Coulis

Season the tomatoes with salt and pepper. Place in a colander. Let stand for 30 minutes to drain excess liquid. Combine the tomatoes, parsley or basil, lemon juice and sugar in a bowl and mix well. Season to taste. Chill, covered, until serving time. May use any fresh herb or combination of fresh herbs. Yield: 1 cup.

1   pound tomatoes, peeled, seeded, finely chopped
    Salt and pepper to taste
2   tablespoons chopped fresh parsley or basil
    Juice of 1/2 lemon
    Pinch of sugar

# Watercress, Cream Cheese and Tomato Roulade

Line an 8x12-inch jelly roll pan with parchment paper; spray with nonstick cooking spray. Combine the watercress, parsley, Parmesan cheese and egg yolks in a bowl and mix well. Season as desired. Beat the egg whites in a mixer bowl until stiff peaks form. Fold into the watercress mixture. Spread in the prepared baking pan. Bake at 375 degrees for 10 to 12 minutes. Let stand until cool. Beat the cream cheese with enough milk in a bowl until of the desired consistency. Add the tomatoes, salt and pepper. Peel the parchment paper from the roulade. Place on an additional sheet of parchment paper on a pan. Spread with the cream cheese mixture. Roll as for a jelly roll. Chill in the refrigerator. Trim the edges and cut into 20 rolls. Yield: 10 (2-roll) servings.

1   bunch watercress, stems removed, chopped
1   tablespoon minced fresh parsley
1   tablespoon grated Parmesan cheese
2   egg yolks
    Salt and freshly ground pepper to taste
2   egg whites
8   ounces cream cheese, softened
    Milk
2   tomatoes, peeled, seeded, chopped

# Downtown
# Soups & Salads

## Chapel

*Every city is justly proud of its houses of worship, but few can boast the combination of fascinating history and beautiful architecture that Savannah claims. For instance, the Temple Mickve Israel is the only known synagogue in the world to be built in the cruciform style. It is the oldest Reform congregation in the U.S., and its archives still contain the original deerskin Torah brought with the 1733 settlers.*

*Christ Episcopal Church was founded in 1733, making it the oldest of Georgia's congregations, while the First African Baptist Church (1788) can claim the oldest black congregation in North America. Here, at the church building built by slaves, are pews hand carved and signed with African tribal symbols. Here also are holes in the floor that ventilate a secret crawl space used as a stop on the Underground Railroad.*

*At Independent Presbyterian Church, Woodrow Wilson was married to Ellen Axson in the manse; at the church on Troup Square, the organist, James Pierpont, wrote a little holiday tune called "Jingle Bells" that became one of the best-selling songs of all time.*

*The church spires depicted here are those of the Cathedral of St. John the Baptist, built in the French Gothic style and dating from 1873 when the cornerstone was laid. The original Cathedral burned in 1898 and the present building, which seats 1,000, was completed and dedicated in 1900.*

# Soups & Salads

Chapel  *by Leslie A. Gibson*
*Illustration Graduate Student, The Savannah College of Art and Design*

# Black Bean Chili with Pineapple Salsa

For the salsa, mix the mint leaves with the lime juice in a bowl. Add the pineapple and mix well. Chill until serving time. Rinse and sort the beans. Soak in water to cover in a bowl overnight. For the chili, cut the beef tips into 1/2-inch pieces. Sprinkle the beef with salt and pepper to taste. Brown in 1 tablespoon oil in a heavy saucepan. Drain and rinse the beans; add to the beef with just enough water to cover. Add the bay leaf, parsley, basil, cilantro, oregano, cumin and cayenne and mix well. Bring to a boil and reduce the heat to low. Sauté the garlic, onion and green pepper in 1 tablespoon oil in a skillet until tender. Add to the chili with the jalapeños, tomato sauce and 1/2 teaspoon salt. Simmer for 1 hour or until the beans are tender. Discard the bay leaf. Serve with the pineapple salsa. The salsa recipe makes 3 cups and can be halved if preferred.
Yield: 4 to 6 servings.

| | |
|---|---|
| 1 | tablespoon chopped mint leaves |
| | Juice of 1 lime |
| 1 | pineapple, coarsely chopped |
| 8 | ounces dried black beans |
| 1 | pound beef tips |
| | Salt and pepper to taste |
| 1 | tablespoon vegetable oil |
| 1 | bay leaf |
| 1 | tablespoon each chopped fresh parsley, basil, cilantro and oregano, or 1 teaspoon dried |
| 3/4 | teaspoon cumin seeds |
| 1/4 | teaspoon cayenne, or to taste |
| 3 | or 4 cloves of garlic, minced |
| 1 | medium onion, chopped |
| 1 | medium green bell pepper, chopped |
| 1 | tablespoon vegetable oil |
| 1 | (2-ounce) can chopped jalapeños |
| 1 | (8-ounce) can tomato sauce |
| 1/2 | teaspoon salt |

# Cream of Brie Soup

Sauté the onion and celery in the butter in a stockpot until tender. Stir in the flour. Cook until bubbly, stirring constantly; remove from the heat. Stir in the milk and chicken stock gradually. Cook until thickened, stirring constantly. Trim and cube cheese. Add to milk mixture. Cook until cheese is melted, stirring constantly. Season with salt and pepper. Ladle into soup bowls. Garnish servings with chopped chives. Yield: 6 servings.

| | |
|---|---|
| 1/2 | cup chopped yellow onion |
| 1/2 | cup sliced celery |
| 1/4 | cup butter |
| 1/4 | cup flour |
| 2 | cups milk |
| 2 | cups chicken stock |
| 12 | ounces Brie cheese |
| | Salt and pepper to taste |
| | Chopped chives (optional) |

# Herbed Tomato Soup

3 medium onions, chopped
¼ cup extra-virgin olive oil
4 medium tomatoes, chopped
3 cloves of garlic, minced
1 bay leaf
1 teaspoon thyme
¼ teaspoon marjoram
2 teaspoons salt
¼ teaspoon pepper
8 cups water
8 slices French bread, toasted
½ cup grated Parmesan cheese

*This is a light soup. The French bread makes it a little different.*

Sauté the onions in olive oil in a large heavy saucepan until light brown. Add the tomatoes. Cook for 5 minutes. Increase the heat to high. Add the garlic, bay leaf, thyme, marjoram, salt, pepper and water. Bring to a boil and reduce the heat. Simmer for 15 minutes. Discard the bay leaf. Process the soup 2 cups at a time in a blender until smooth. Return to the saucepan and bring to a boil. Place 2 slices of toasted bread in each serving bowl. Ladle the soup over the bread. Sprinkle with the cheese. Yield: 4 servings.

# White Gazpacho

3 medium cucumbers, peeled, coarsely chopped
3 cups cooled chicken broth
3 cups sour cream
3 tablespoons white vinegar
1 clove of garlic, crushed
2 teaspoons salt
2 tomatoes, peeled, chopped
½ cup sliced green onions
½ cup chopped parsley
¾ cup toasted chopped almonds

*A fun way to serve an old standby and delicious, too!*

Process the cucumbers with half the chicken broth in the blender for 1 minute. Combine the remaining chicken broth, sour cream, vinegar, garlic and salt in a bowl. Add the cucumber purée and mix well. Chill until serving time. Ladle into serving bowls. Sprinkle with the tomatoes, green onions, parsley and almonds.
Yield: 6 to 8 servings.

# Beefy Vegetable Soup

Brown the ground beef in a saucepan, stirring until crumbly; drain. Add the water, tomato sauce, tomatoes, garlic, sugar, salt and pepper and mix well. Add the vegetables. Simmer for several hours or until of the desired consistency.
Yield: 6 servings.

1    *pound ground beef or turkey*
2    *cups water*
1    *(8-ounce) can tomato sauce*
2    *(16-ounce) cans stewed tomatoes*
     *Minced garlic to taste*
1    *teaspoon sugar*
2    *teaspoons salt*
     *Pepper to taste*
     *Chopped fresh vegetables of choice, such as carrots, onions, green beans or zucchini*

# Italian Sausage Soup with Tortellini

Remove the casing from the sausage. Brown in a saucepan, stirring until crumbly; drain and set aside. Sauté the onion and garlic in a large nonstick saucepan until tender. Add the beef broth, water, wine, tomatoes, carrots, tomato sauce, basil, oregano and sausage. Simmer, covered, for 30 minutes; skim the surface. Stir in the parsley, green pepper and tortellini. Simmer, covered, for 35 to 40 minutes or until the pasta is tender. Ladle into soup bowls. Garnish the servings with Parmesan cheese. Yield: 8 servings.

1    *pound Italian sausage*
1    *cup coarsely chopped onion*
2    *cloves of garlic, minced*
5    *cups beef broth*
1/2   *cup water*
1    *cup dry red wine*
2    *cups chopped peeled tomatoes*
1    *cup sliced carrots*
1    *(8-ounce) can tomato sauce*
1/2   *teaspoon basil*
3/4   *teaspoon oregano*
3    *tablespoons chopped parsley*
1    *medium green bell pepper, chopped*
2    *cups fresh or frozen tortellini*

# Cream of Mushroom Soup

1    *pound fresh mushrooms, sliced*
1/2  *cup finely chopped onion*
1/4  *cup butter*
3    *tablespoons flour*
1 1/4 *cups chicken stock or*
      *1 (10-ounce) can chicken broth*
1    *tablespoon dry sherry*
1    *teaspoon tarragon*
1    *teaspoon salt*
1/4  *teaspoon pepper*
2    *cups half-and-half*

Sauté the mushrooms and onion in half the butter in a large skillet for 5 to 7 minutes, stirring frequently. Melt the remaining butter in a large saucepan. Stir in the flour. Cook until light brown, stirring constantly; remove from the heat. Add the chicken stock, wine, tarragon, salt, pepper and mushroom mixture. Cook until thickened, stirring constantly. Simmer for 20 minutes. Stir in the half-and-half. Cook just until heated through; do not boil. Yield: 6 to 8 servings.

# Potato and Onion Soup with Roquefort Cheese

2    *medium-large onions,*
      *thinly sliced*
1/2  *teaspoon minced garlic*
3    *tablespoons unsalted butter*
3    *medium potatoes, peeled, cut*
      *into 1-inch pieces*
2    *cups light chicken stock or low-*
      *sodium broth*
3 1/2 *to 4 ounces Roquefort or bleu*
      *cheese, crumbled*
1/2  *teaspoon salt*
1/4  *teaspoon pepper*
1    *cup light cream*
1/3  *cup whipping cream*

*This can also be made with bleu cheese. It can be served cold.*

Sauté the onions and garlic in the butter in a large heavy nonreactive saucepan until the onions are tender but not brown. Add the potatoes and stir to coat well. Cook for 5 minutes. Stir in the chicken stock. Bring to a boil and reduce the heat. Cook for 20 minutes or until the potatoes are tender. Cool to room temperature. Combine with the Roquefort cheese, salt and pepper in a blender; process until smooth. Combine with the light cream and whipping cream in a saucepan. Cook until heated through; do not boil. Ladle into soup bowls. Garnish with freshly grated pepper or homemade croutons. Yield: 5 servings.

# Fish Stew

Drain the clams, reserving the liquid. Sauté the onion, green pepper and garlic in the olive oil in a stockpot until tender but not brown. Add the reserved clam liquid, tomatoes, tomato purée, wine, basil, salt and pepper. Simmer, covered, for 10 minutes. Add the fish. Simmer, covered, for 20 minutes. Add the drained clams, shrimp and parsley. Cook just until the shrimp are tender. Serve in deep bowls with crusty bread. You may add other kinds of seafood, such as lobster, scallops or oysters. Yield: 4 to 6 servings.

1   (5-ounce) can whole clams
1   cup chopped onion
1   cup chopped green bell pepper
2   cloves of garlic, minced
1/4  cup olive oil or vegetable oil
1   (28-ounce) can tomatoes
1   (15-ounce) can tomato purée
1   cup red wine
1/2  teaspoon basil, crumbled
1 1/2  teaspoons salt
1/4  teaspoon pepper
1   pound thawed frozen halibut or fresh fish, cut into serving portions
8   ounces fresh or frozen shrimp, peeled, deveined
1/4  cup chopped parsley

# Low-Country Crab Stew

Shred the crab meat, discarding bits of shell. Sauté the onions in the butter in a large saucepan over low heat until tender. Add the crab meat, half-and-half, Tabasco sauce, salt and cayenne. Simmer just until heated through; do not boil.
Yield: 6 servings.

1   pint crab meat
2   medium onions, finely chopped
6   tablespoons butter
4   cups half-and-half
3   drops of Tabasco sauce
1   teaspoon salt
1/2  teaspoon cayenne

# Seafood Chowder

1½ pounds crab meat
1 pound shrimp, peeled, deveined
8 ounces grouper or other white
 fish, cut into bite-size pieces
¼ cup butter
1 large Vidalia onion, chopped
4 cups milk
2 cups whipping cream
1 teaspoon salt
⅓ cup sherry

*This can also be served over rice as an entrée.*

Sauté the crab meat, shrimp and fish in the butter in a skillet for 5 minutes. Add the onion. Sauté until the onion is tender but not brown. Combine the milk and cream in a large microwave-safe bowl. Microwave on Medium until warm. Add the seafood mixture and mix well. Microwave until heated through, stirring frequently. Stir in the salt and wine. Ladle into serving bowls. Garnish the servings with croutons. The flavor improves if chilled and reheated. Yield: 6 servings.

# Bing Cherry Mold

1 (16-ounce) can Bing cherries
½ cup port
½ cup orange juice
1 package black cherry gelatin
3 ounces cream cheese, crumbled

*You must use Bing cherries in this recipe. The Bing cherries and black cherry gelatin can be challenging to find, but worth the search.*

Drain the cherries, reserving 1 cup juice. Cut the cherries into halves, discarding the pits. Heat the reserved cherry juice with the wine and orange juice in a saucepan. Add the gelatin, stirring to dissolve completely. Stir in the cherries. Grease 8 to 10 individual molds or 1 large salad mold with mayonnaise. Spoon in the gelatin mixture. Stir in the cream cheese. Chill until set. Unmold onto a serving plate lined with Bibb lettuce. Garnish with dollops of mayonnaise. Yield: 8 to 10 servings.

# Grated Cucumber Salad Ring

*Use hydroponically grown cucumbers in the winter for a nice summer taste all year.*

Dissolve the gelatin in the boiling water in a mixer bowl. Add the cream cheese, salad dressing, horseradish and salt; beat until smooth. Stir in the lemon juice. Chill until partially set. Stir in the cucumbers and green onions. Spoon into a 4-cup ring mold. Chill until firm. Unmold onto a serving plate to serve. Yield: 8 servings.

| | |
|---|---|
| 1 | package lime gelatin |
| 3/4 | cup boiling water |
| 6 | ounces cream cheese, softened |
| 1 | cup mayonnaise-type salad dressing |
| 1 | teaspoon horseradish |
| 1/4 | teaspoon salt |
| 2 | tablespoons lemon juice |
| 3/4 | cup grated peeled cucumbers, drained |
| 1/4 | cup grated green onions |

# Lemon Cream Salad

Mix the gelatin, sugar and salt in a bowl. Add the boiling water, stirring for 2 minutes or until the gelatin mixture dissolves completely. Stir in the lemonade concentrate. Chill just until the gelatin begins to set around the edge. Fold in the whipped cream. Spoon into a 4-cup mold or individual molds. Chill until set. Unmold onto a serving plate. Arrange fresh fruit around the mold. Garnish with fresh mint. Yield: 8 to 10 servings.

| | |
|---|---|
| 1 | (3-ounce) package lemon gelatin |
| 1/3 | cup sugar |
| 1/8 | teaspoon salt |
| 1 | cup boiling water |
| 1 | (6-ounce) can frozen lemonade concentrate, thawed |
| 1 | cup whipping cream, whipped |
| | Fresh fruit in season, such as strawberries, blueberries, raspberries, cantaloupe, honeydew melon, red grapes or watermelon |
| | Fresh mint (optional) |

# Peach Aspic

1   envelope unflavored gelatin
1/4   cup cold water
2   (3-ounce) packages peach
    gelatin
1 1/4 cups boiling water
1   cup orange juice
3   tablespoons freshly squeezed
    lemon juice
1   tablespoon grated lemon peel
1 1/2 cups puréed fresh or frozen
    peaches
3   to 4 tablespoons sugar
    (optional)
3   ounces cream cheese, softened
1   tablespoon mayonnaise
1   peach, puréed

Use fresh peaches when they are available for this pretty dish, which can be served as a light dessert or salad.

Soften the unflavored gelatin in the cold water in a bowl. Add the peach gelatin. Add the boiling water, stirring to dissolve the gelatins completely. Stir in the orange juice, lemon juice, lemon peel, 1 1/2 cups peach purée and sugar. Spoon into a 1 1/2-quart mold. Chill until set. Blend the cream cheese and mayonnaise in a bowl. Add puréed peaches and mix well. Unmold the salad onto a serving plate. Serve with the cream cheese dressing. Yield: 6 servings.

# Crunchy Bok Choy

2   packages ramen noodles
1   package sunflower seeds
1   package slivered almonds
    Melted butter
1   large head bok choy, chopped
12   green onions, chopped
1/4   cup cider vinegar
1/4   cup vegetable oil
2   tablespoons soy sauce
1/4   cup sugar

This can be made with a mixture of purple and green cabbages. It is good for a picnic.

Break the ramen noodles into a 9x13-inch baking dish, discarding the seasoning packet. Add the sunflower seeds and almonds. Drizzle with melted butter. Roast at 300 degrees for 20 minutes. Cool to room temperature. Combine with the bok choy and green onions in a large bowl. For the dressing, combine the vinegar, oil, soy sauce and sugar in a small bowl and whisk to mix well. Add to the salad and mix gently. Yield: 12 servings.

# Broccoli Slaw

Mix the broccoli, celery and green onions in a large bowl. For the dressing, combine the sunflower oil, soy sauce, vinegar and sugar in a covered jar and shake to mix well. Add to the salad and toss lightly. Chill until serving time. Add the almonds, sunflower seeds and rice noodles just before serving; toss gently. Yield: 8 to 10 servings.

1 package broccoli slaw
3 ribs celery, chopped
4 or 5 green onions, chopped
1/2 cup sunflower oil
2 teaspoons soy sauce
1/4 cup white vinegar
1/2 cup sugar
3/4 cup sliced almonds
1/2 cup sunflower seeds
1 can rice noodles

# Garlic and Bleu Cheese Salad

For the dressing, combine the canola oil, vinegar, garlic, sugar, salt and pepper in a bowl and mix well. Chill thoroughly. Sprinkle the avocado with lemon juice to prevent browning. Combine the romaine lettuce, Bibb lettuce, tomato and onion in a large bowl. Add the avocado and mix gently. Add the bleu cheese, bacon and dressing 10 minutes before serving, tossing to mix. Yield: 8 servings.

3/4 cup canola oil
1/3 cup apple cider vinegar
1 large clove of garlic, minced
4 to 5 teaspoons sugar
1/2 teaspoon salt
Pepper to taste
1 large avocado, sliced
Lemon juice
1 head romaine lettuce, torn
1 head Bibb lettuce, torn (optional)
1 large tomato or 6 Roma tomatoes, coarsely chopped
1 medium Vidalia or purple onion, sliced
4 ounces bleu cheese, crumbled
8 ounces bacon, crisp-fried, broken into 1/2-inch pieces

# Chèvre Salad

2  tablespoons red wine vinegar
1/4  cup olive oil
1  teaspoon Dijon mustard
5¹/2  ounces chèvre, cut into 16 slices
16  slices baguette
   Butter
   Salad greens

For the dressing, combine the vinegar, olive oil and mustard in a bowl and mix well. Place the cheese slices on the slices of bread. Sauté the bottoms of the bread slices lightly in butter in a skillet. Place on a baking sheet. Toast in the oven just until the cheese melts. Add the dressing to the salad greens in a bowl and toss lightly. Spoon onto serving plates. Top each serving with 3 or 4 cheese toasts. Yield: 5 or 6 servings.

# Gorgonzola and Pecan Crunch Salad

1  teaspoon Dijon mustard
2  teaspoons honey
2  tablespoons red wine vinegar
1/4  cup orange juice
1  teaspoon grated orange zest
1/4  cup hazelnut oil
1/4  cup light olive oil
2/3  cup chopped pecans
1  tablespoon sugar
1/2  teaspoon salt
   Cayenne and pepper to taste
2  tablespoons butter
7  cups mixed lettuces
6  ounces Gorgonzola cheese,
   crumbled

For the vinaigrette, combine the mustard, honey, vinegar, orange juice and orange zest in a small bowl and mix well. Whisk in the hazelnut oil and olive oil. Chill until serving time. For the pecan crunch, combine the pecans, sugar, salt, cayenne, pepper and butter in a small saucepan. Cook until the sugar caramelizes, stirring constantly. Place in a small nonrecycled paper bag. Let stand until cool, shaking occasionally to break into pieces. Combine with the lettuces and cheese in a salad bowl. Add the dressing just before serving and toss lightly. Yield: 6 servings.

# Greens Scarborough

For the dressing, whisk the olive oil, vinegar, salt and pepper in a bowl. Chill for 1 hour or longer. Combine the romaine lettuce, iceberg lettuce, grapes, almonds and cheese in a salad bowl. Add the dressing at serving time and toss lightly. Yield: 6 to 8 servings.

*1/2 cup olive oil*
*1/4 cup white wine vinegar*
*Salt to taste*
*1/4 teaspoon pepper*
*1 head romaine lettuce, torn*
*1 head iceberg lettuce, torn*
*1 cup grape halves*
*1 small package slivered almonds*
*4 ounces feta cheese, crumbled*

# Fresh Greens with Raspberry Roquefort Vinaigrette

Combine the salad greens, green onions, cranberries and pecans in a large salad bowl. For the dressing, whisk the olive oil, vinegar, salt and pepper in a small bowl. Stir in the cheese. Add to the salad and toss lightly to mix well. Garnish with cherry tomatoes. Serve immediately. Yield: 6 servings.

*8 cups mixed fresh salad greens*
*1/4 cup sliced green onions*
*1/4 cup dried cranberries*
*1/2 cup chopped pecans or walnuts*
*1/2 cup extra-virgin olive oil*
*1/4 cup raspberry vinegar*
*1/4 teaspoon salt*
*1/8 teaspoon pepper*
*1/2 cup crumbled Roquefort cheese*
*Cherry tomatoes (optional)*

# Hearts of Palm and Strawberry Salad

1/3 cup cider vinegar
2 tablespoons lemon juice
3/4 cup sugar
1 teaspoon salt
1 cup light salad oil
1/2 small onion, grated
1 teaspoon dry mustard
1/2 teaspoon paprika
1 1/2 tablespoons poppy seeds
1 1/2 pounds fresh spinach, torn
1 can hearts of palm, drained, chopped
1 pint fresh strawberries, sliced
1 cup chopped walnuts

For the dressing, combine the vinegar, lemon juice, sugar and salt in a saucepan. Heat until the sugar dissolves, stirring frequently. Cool to room temperature. Whisk in the oil, onion, dry mustard, paprika and poppy seeds. Combine the spinach, hearts of palm, strawberries and walnuts in a bowl. Add the desired amount of dressing at serving time and toss lightly. Yield: 12 servings.

# Lentil Salad with Olive Oil Dressing

2 onions
4 whole cloves
1 pound dried lentils
5 cups water
1 bay leaf
1 1/2 teaspoons salt
1 1/2 teaspoons pepper
2/3 cup olive oil
1/4 cup red wine vinegar
1/4 teaspoon dry mustard
1/4 teaspoon sugar
2 cloves of garlic, minced
1/2 teaspoon Worcestershire sauce
Cayenne to taste
1/2 cup chopped scallions
3 tablespoons chopped parsley
Avocado, tomato slices or tomato cups (optional)

Stud each onion with 2 cloves. Rinse and sort the lentils. Combine with the water, onions, bay leaf, salt and pepper in a saucepan. Bring to a boil and reduce the heat. Simmer, covered, for 30 minutes; do not stir. Drain excess liquid. Remove the onions and bay leaf; discard the cloves and bay leaf. For the dressing, combine the onions, olive oil, vinegar, dry mustard, sugar, garlic and Worcestershire sauce in a food processor or blender container and process until smooth. Add cayenne and adjust seasonings. Combine with the lentils in a bowl and mix well. Chill for 6 hours or longer. Add the scallions and parsley just before serving. Garnish with avocado or tomato slices or serve in tomato cups. Yield: 12 servings.

# Pear and Bleu Cheese Salad

For the dressing, whisk together the oil, vinegar, shallots, sugar and salt in a bowl. Place the salad greens on 6 serving plates. Brush the pear slices with lemon juice to prevent browning. Arrange on the salad greens. Sprinkle with the walnuts and bleu cheese. Drizzle with the salad dressing.
Yield: 6 servings.

$1/3$ cup vegetable oil
$2^1/2$ tablespoons raspberry vinegar
1 tablespoon chopped shallots
$1/2$ teaspoon sugar
$1/2$ teaspoon salt
6 to 8 cups mixed baby salad greens
1 red pear, sliced
$1/4$ cup lemon juice
3 ounces walnut halves
4 ounces bleu cheese, crumbled

# River Street Salad

For the dressing, combine the salad oil, olive oil, vinegar, 2 tablespoons lemon juice, garlic, mustard, Worcestershire sauce, salt and pepper in a covered jar and shake to mix well. Chill until serving time. Squeeze the lemon over the avocado slices to prevent browning. Combine the lettuce, watercress, green onions, avocados, chicken, tomato, cheese, bacon and eggs in a large salad bowl. Add the dressing and toss lightly.
Yield: 4 servings.

1 cup salad oil
$1/2$ cup olive oil
$1/2$ cup red wine vinegar
2 tablespoons lemon juice
1 clove of garlic, minced
1 teaspoon Dijon mustard
$1^1/2$ teaspoons Worcestershire sauce
1 teaspoon salt
$1/2$ teaspoon pepper
$1/2$ lemon
2 avocados, sliced
1 head Boston lettuce, torn
$3/4$ to 1 cup watercress
$1/4$ cup chopped green onions
2 cups chopped cooked chicken, chilled
1 tomato, chopped
$3/4$ cup shredded Cheddar cheese
6 slices crisp-fried bacon, crumbled
2 hard-cooked eggs

# Shrimp and Avocado in Mustard Sauce

1   egg yolk or equivalent egg
    substitute
1/4 cup white wine vinegar
2   tablespoons Dijon mustard
1/2 cup olive oil
2   tablespoons chopped parsley
2   tablespoons chopped chives
1   tablespoon sliced scallions
2   large avocados, chopped
    Lemon juice
24  shrimp, cooked

For the dressing, combine the egg yolk, vinegar and mustard in a blender and process until smooth. Add the olive oil gradually, processing constantly until smooth. Stir in the parsley, chives and scallions. Sprinkle the avocados with lemon juice to prevent browning. Cut larger shrimp into halves. Combine the shrimp and avocados in a bowl. Add the dressing and toss lightly. Chill until serving time. For health purposes, pasteurized egg product may be used in place of the egg yolk in the dressing. Yield: 12 servings.

# Crunchy Chutney Chicken Salad

4   large chicken breasts, cooked,
    chopped
3/4 cup low-fat Italian salad
    dressing
3/4 cup chutney
1   (8-ounce) can sliced water
    chestnuts, drained
4   to 8 ounces frozen pea pods,
    thawed
3   ribs celery, finely chopped
2   green onions, chopped
    (optional)
1   tablespoon Durkee sauce
    Mayonnaise or low-fat
    mayonnaise

*Water chestnuts and chutney give this chicken salad a new twist.*

Combine the chicken and salad dressing in a bowl and mix well. Marinate in the refrigerator for 1 hour or longer. Add the chutney, water chestnuts, pea pods, celery, green onions and Durkee sauce and mix well. Add enough mayonnaise to moisten. Chill for 1 hour or longer. Yield: 6 to 8 servings.

# Oglethorpe Salad with Balsamic Dressing

*The secret to this wonderful salad is to make the dressing in the skillet in which the chicken was cooked—deglazing with balsamic vinegar!*

Rinse the chicken and pat dry. Pound with the broad side of a chef's knife and set aside. Arrange the lettuce in the center of 4 serving plates. Place the endive around the edge. Arrange the red pepper spoke fashion over the lettuce. Coat the chicken with a mixture of flour, salt and pepper. Sauté in the olive oil in a skillet for 3 to 4 minutes on each side or until cooked through. Remove the chicken from the skillet, reserving the pan drippings in the skillet. Slice the chicken into strips and arrange in spokes between the pepper strips. Add the scallions to the skillet. Sauté lightly. Add the vinegar, stirring to deglaze the skillet. Drizzle over the salads. Yield: 4 servings.

4   boneless skinless chicken breasts
1   bunch red leaf lettuce
1   bunch green leaf lettuce
1   bunch radicchio
2   or 3 Belgian endives
1   large red bell pepper, sliced into thin strips
3   tablespoons flour
1/2   teaspoon salt
1/2   teaspoon pepper
3   to 4 tablespoons olive oil
1/2   cup sliced scallions
2   tablespoons (or more) balsamic vinegar

# Chicken and Mango Pasta Salad

For the dressing, combine the chutney, sour cream, mayonnaise, honey, ginger, curry powder and salt in a bowl and mix well. Let stand at room temperature. Cook the pasta using the package directions; drain, rinse with cold water and drain again. Combine the pasta with the chicken and 1 cup of the dressing in a bowl; toss lightly. Add the celery, green pepper, half the grapes and 1/2 cup of the almonds and mix well. Chill in the refrigerator. Let stand at room temperature for 30 minutes before serving. Drizzle with the remaining dressing at serving time. Top with the remaining grapes and almonds. Yield: 6 servings.

1/2   cup mango chutney
1   cup sour cream
1/4   cup mayonnaise
1   tablespoon honey
1 1/2   teaspoons freshly grated ginger
1   teaspoon curry powder
1/2   teaspoon salt
12   ounces fusilli
2   cups chopped cooked chicken
1/2   cup thinly sliced celery
1/4   cup chopped green bell pepper
1   cup red grape halves
3/4   cup toasted slivered almonds

# Orzo Salad Florentine

1   (16-ounce) package orzo
    Chicken stock
2   tablespoons olive oil
1   cup julienned fresh basil
1½  cups crumbled feta cheese
¾   cup toasted pine nuts
1   bunch green onions, chopped
1   bunch fresh spinach, julienned
1½  teaspoons lemon juice
¼   cup olive oil
    Salt and cracked pepper to taste

Cook the orzo using the package directions, substituting chicken stock for the water. Drain well and toss with 2 tablespoons olive oil. Combine with the basil, cheese, pine nuts, green onions and spinach in a large bowl and mix gently. Whisk the lemon juice and ¼ cup olive oil in a bowl. Toss with the salad. Season with the salt and pepper. Yield: 6 servings.

# Pasta Seafood Salad

24  ounces fusilli, cooked, drained,
    cooled
½   cup chopped green onions
12  ounces shrimp, cooked, peeled
12  ounces crab meat, cooked
½   cup chopped green bell pepper
½   cup chopped red bell pepper
1   cup mayonnaise
¼   cup lemon juice
4   drops of Tabasco sauce
    Salt to taste
    Romaine lettuce leaves
4   to 6 teaspoons chopped green
    onions
    Parsley, lemon and strawberries
    (optional)

Combine the pasta, ½ cup green onions, shrimp, crab meat, green pepper and red pepper in a large bowl and toss to mix. Add a mixture of the mayonnaise, lemon juice and Tabasco sauce and toss gently. Season with the salt. Serve over the lettuce on individual plates. Top with 4 to 6 teaspoons green onions. Garnish with fresh parsley, lemon wedges and strawberries. Yield: 4 servings.

# Sweet-and-Sour Ramen Noodle Salad

Combine the oil, vinegar, soy sauce and sugar in a covered jar; shake well to mix. Brown the ramen noodles and walnuts in the butter in a skillet; drain on paper towels. Toss the lettuce, broccoli, green onions and noodle mixture in a large bowl. Add the dressing and toss lightly. Yield: 4 to 6 servings.

| | |
|---|---|
| 1 | cup vegetable oil |
| 1/3 | cup red wine vinegar |
| 3 | tablespoons soy sauce |
| 3/4 | cup sugar |
| 1 | package ramen noodles |
| 1 | cup chopped walnuts |
| 1/2 | cup butter |
| 2 | bunches romaine lettuce, torn into bite-size pieces |
| 1 | head broccoli, finely chopped |
| 1 | bunch green onions, chopped |

# Tomato, Basil and Feta Rigatoni

*Try this wonderful salad with fresh summer yellow squash, zucchini, broccoli, cauliflower, snow peas or pea pods, or as a main dish with the addition of cooked chicken or shrimp.*

Combine the garlic, tomatoes, basil and olive oil in a bowl. Let stand for 1 hour. Cook the pasta using the package directions and drain well. Stir the vinegar into the tomato mixture. Toss with the pasta in a large bowl. Crumble the cheese over the top. May add chopped walnuts and niçoise olives. Yield: 4 servings.

| | |
|---|---|
| 1 | medium clove of garlic, finely chopped |
| 4 | medium tomatoes, coarsely chopped |
| 1/2 | cup chopped fresh basil |
| 3/4 | cup olive oil |
| 1 | (16-ounce) package rigatoni, fusilli or tricolor pasta |
| 1 | tablespoon balsamic vinegar, or to taste |
| 12 | ounces feta cheese, crumbled |
| | Chopped walnuts (optional) |
| | Niçoise olives (optional) |

# Downtown Entrées

## Traci's Window

*It doesn't take much to realize the beauty of the building materials that
make up Savannah's Historic District—a short walk around the block
will do. Terra cotta, ironwork, brownstone, clapboard—all contribute to the
unique play of light and shadow, which creates the lovely texture of time
on Savannah's streetscapes.*

*But no building material can match the importance of Savannah gray bricks.
They are used for buildings, garden paths, chimneys, stairways, walls—
bare to the elements or covered with peeling stucco, creeping fig, or ivy.
These handmade, mellow old bricks are the heart of Savannah's infrastructure
as much as the moss-draped live oaks are the basis of the dreaming landscape.*

*However, before the preservation movement began in earnest in 1955,
building contractors had discovered that the Savannah grays were highly prized
and unable to be duplicated, and that many historic buildings were worth more
when demolished than intact. Partially because of this, the number of
historic buildings razed increased dramatically as prosperous times returned
after World War II. In the suburbs, new homes of Savannah gray brick
became a mark of distinction.*

*Today, in downtown Savannah, follow the low murmur of conversation and
the clink of ice in glasses, and chances are you'll find a hostess and her guests in
a hidden garden on a terrace of, and surrounded by walls of, the lovely
and elegant Savannah grays.*

*The illustration shows the beautiful juxtaposition of building materials on a
Gaston Street house—brick, terra cotta, stucco, brownstone—and shutters
creating a dim, cool escape from the Savannah sun.*

# Entrées

Traci's Window  by Charlotte Haynes Pickering
Illustration Undergraduate Student, The Savannah College of Art and Design

# Chatham Rib-Eye Roast

Place the roast in a shallow dish. Pour a mixture of the red wine, oil, green onions, celery, green pepper, white vinegar, salad dressing mix and Worcestershire sauce over the roast, turning to coat. Marinate, covered, in the refrigerator for 8 hours, turning occasionally. Drain the roast, discarding the marinade. Place the roast in a baking pan. Insert a meat thermometer into the thickest portion of the roast. Bake in a moderate oven for 2 hours or until the meat thermometer registers 140 degrees for rare or 160 degrees for medium. Yield: 12 to 15 servings.

| | |
|---|---|
| 1 | (5- to 6-pound) boneless rib-eye roast, trimmed |
| 1/2 | cup dry red wine |
| 1/4 | cup vegetable oil |
| 1/3 | cup chopped green onions |
| 1/3 | cup chopped celery |
| 1/4 | cup chopped green bell pepper |
| 3 | tablespoons white vinegar |
| 1 | envelope Italian salad dressing mix |
| 1 1/2 | teaspoons Worcestershire sauce |

# Marinated Flank Steak

*To reduce clean up, marinate the steaks in a large sealable plastic bag. Any leftover steak makes a great steak salad.*

Pierce both sides of the steaks with a fork. Place in a 9x13-inch dish. Pour a mixture of the soy sauce, Pickapeppa sauce, Worcestershire sauce, olive oil, wine, wine vinegar, brown sugar and garlic over the steaks, turning to coat. Marinate, covered, in the refrigerator for 24 hours, turning occasionally. Drain, discarding the marinade. Grill the steaks over hot coals for 4 to 5 minutes or until done to taste. Cut the steaks cross grain into thin slices. Yield: 6 to 8 servings.

| | |
|---|---|
| 2 | (1 1/4-pound) flank steaks |
| 1/2 | cup soy sauce |
| 1/4 | cup Pickapeppa sauce |
| 1/4 | cup Worcestershire sauce |
| 3 | tablespoons olive oil |
| 3 | tablespoons burgundy or other dry red wine |
| 3 | tablespoons red wine vinegar |
| 2 1/2 | tablespoons brown sugar |
| 2 | cloves of garlic, minced |

# London Broil

1  (12-ounce) can beer
1/2  cup peanut oil
2  tablespoons orange marmalade
1  tablespoon sugar
1  teaspoon dry mustard
1  teaspoon ginger
1  teaspoon Worcestershire sauce
1  teaspoon garlic powder
   Salt and pepper to taste
1  (3-pound) London broil

*May be broiled or grilled.*

Combine the beer, peanut oil, orange marmalade, sugar, dry mustard, ginger, Worcestershire sauce, garlic powder, salt and pepper in a bowl and mix well. Pour over the beef in a sealable plastic bag, turning to coat. Marinate in the refrigerator for 24 hours, turning occasionally. Drain, reserving the marinade. Grill over hot coals until done to taste, basting with the reserved marinade.
Yield: 4 to 6 servings.

# New Neighbor Spaghetti

8  ounces spaghetti or noodles
1 1/2  pounds ground round steak or ground chuck
1  (28-ounce) jar spaghetti sauce with mushrooms or vegetables
1  (16-ounce) can Hunt's Special tomato sauce
   Garlic salt or garlic powder to taste (optional)
2  cups sour cream
8  ounces cream cheese, softened
1  medium onion, chopped
1  green bell pepper, chopped
   Shredded Cheddar cheese

Cook the spaghetti in a saucepan using package directions until al dente; drain and rinse. Brown the ground steak in a skillet, stirring until crumbly; drain. Add the spaghetti sauce, tomato sauce and garlic salt and mix well. Simmer until heated through, stirring occasionally. Combine the sour cream, cream cheese, onion and green pepper in a bowl and mix well. Layer 1/3 of the spaghetti, 1/2 of the ground steak mixture, 1/2 of the remaining spaghetti, cream cheese mixture, remaining spaghetti and remaining ground steak mixture in a 2 1/2-quart baking dish. Sprinkle with Cheddar cheese. Chill, covered, for several hours. Bake at 350 degrees for 50 to 60 minutes or until brown and bubbly. May substitute low-fat or nonfat products for the spaghetti sauce, sour cream, cream cheese and Cheddar cheese.
Yield: 8 servings.

# Elegant Beef Tenderloin

Combine the sherry, olive oil, soy sauce, garlic and pepper in a bowl and mix well. Pour over the tenderloin in a shallow baking dish, turning to coat. Marinate, covered, for 8 hours to overnight, turning occasionally. Bake, uncovered, at 425 degrees for 20 minutes for medium-rare. Grill over hot coals until done to taste.
Yield: 18 to 20 servings.

1    cup cream sherry
1    cup olive oil
1    cup soy sauce
1    clove of garlic, minced
    Freshly ground pepper to taste
1    (6-pound) beef tenderloin, trimmed

# Basil-Tarragon Veal Chops

Combine 2 tablespoons olive oil, scallions, wine vinegar, parsley, garlic and 1/2 teaspoon pepper in a bowl and mix well. Add the veal chops, turning to coat. Marinate, covered, in the refrigerator for 24 hours, turning 3 or 4 times. Let stand until room temperature. Brown the chops in 3 tablespoons olive oil in a large skillet. Place each chop on a 12x12-inch piece of foil. Sprinkle both sides with basil, tarragon, 1/4 teaspoon pepper and salt; seal. Bake at 325 degrees for 30 minutes or until tender.
Yield: 4 servings.

5    tablespoons extra-virgin olive oil, divided
2    tablespoons minced scallions
1    tablespoon red wine vinegar
1    tablespoon chopped fresh parsley
1    clove of garlic, crushed
1/2   teaspoon cracked pepper
4    lean loin veal chops
1/2   teaspoon basil
1/2   teaspoon tarragon
1/4   teaspoon cracked pepper
    Salt to taste

# Veal Marsala

8 ounces veal scallopini
Salt and freshly ground pepper
to taste
Flour
1/4 cup olive oil
1 tablespoon minced shallot
1/2 cup marsala
1/4 cup chopped fresh basil
2 tablespoons Dijon mustard
2 tablespoons unsalted butter

Pound the veal 1/4 inch thick between sheets of waxed paper. Season both sides with salt and pepper. Coat with flour; shake off excess. Heat the olive oil in a skillet over medium-high heat until hot. Add the veal. Sauté for 2 minutes on each side. Remove to a serving platter; cover to keep warm. Sauté the shallot in the pan drippings in the skillet until tender. Deglaze the skillet with the wine. Cook until reduced by 1/2, stirring frequently. Stir in the basil and Dijon mustard. Remove from heat. Whisk in the butter. Drizzle over the veal. Yield: 2 servings.

# Roasted Lamb Chops with Crumb Coating

4 lamb chops, sliced 1 1/4 inches
thick
Salt and black pepper to taste
1/2 cup dry bread crumbs
1/2 cup chopped fresh parsley
2 large cloves of garlic
1 large shallot, minced
3 tablespoons melted butter
1 teaspoon dry mustard
1/8 teaspoon cayenne

Season the lamb chops with salt and black pepper. Process the bread crumbs, parsley, garlic and shallot in a food processor until very fine. Transfer to a shallow dish. Combine the butter, dry mustard and cayenne in a shallow dish and mix well. Dip the lamb chops in the butter mixture; coat with the bread crumb mixture. Arrange on a rack in a shallow baking pan. Roast at 500 degrees for 16 minutes or until golden brown and done to taste. Yield: 2 (2-lamb chop) servings.

# Lamb Chops Tarragon

Pat the peppercorns into both sides of the lamb chops. Sauté in the olive oil in a skillet for 10 minutes per side for medium or until done to taste. Add the bouillon, lime juice and butter. Simmer for 5 minutes, stirring occasionally. Stir in the tarragon and lime zest. Simmer for 5 minutes longer, stirring frequently. Remove lamb chops to a serving platter. Drizzle with the sauce.
Yield: 4 servings.

$1^1/2$ tablespoons black peppercorns
4 lamb chops
$^1/4$ cup olive oil
$^1/4$ cup beef bouillon
$^1/4$ cup fresh lime juice
1 tablespoon butter
1 tablespoon chopped fresh tarragon, or 2 teaspoons dried tarragon
Zest of 1 lime

# Marinated Leg of Lamb

*Must be prepared in advance.*

Split the leg of lamb down the center cutting to but not completely through. Place in a large shallow dish. Combine the Dijon mustard, soy sauce, rosemary, gingerroot, garlic, salt and olive oil in a bowl and mix well. Pour over the lamb, turning to coat. Marinate in the refrigerator overnight. Grill over hot coals or until a meat thermometer inserted in the center registers 140 degrees. Let lamb stand for 15 minutes before serving. May broil lamb on a rack in a broiler pan for 10 minutes on each side. Place the oven rack in the upper $^1/3$ of the oven. Roast at 375 degrees for 15 minutes. May reheat in the microwave.
Yield: 10 to 12 servings.

1 (5-pound) leg of lamb, boned
8 ounces Dijon mustard
3 tablespoons soy sauce
2 tablespoons rosemary
2 tablespoons grated fresh ginger
2 cloves of garlic, minced
$^1/2$ teaspoon salt
2 tablespoons olive oil

# Fettuccini Florentine

12  ounces fettuccini
1   (10-ounce) package frozen
    chopped spinach
3   tablespoons olive oil
1   small onion, thinly sliced
1   cup milk
2   cups ricotta cheese
1   teaspoon salt
2   tablespoons slivered cooked ham
    Freshly grated Parmesan cheese
    Freshly ground pepper

Cook fettuccini using package directions; drain. Return the pasta to the saucepan and cover to keep warm. Combine the spinach with enough boiling water to cover in a bowl. Let stand for 5 minutes to thaw; drain and squeeze the moisture from the spinach. Heat the olive oil in a 10-inch skillet until hot. Sauté the onion in the prepared skillet until tender. Add the spinach. Cook for 3 to 5 minutes or until heated through, stirring frequently. Add the spinach mixture to the fettuccini and mix well. Stir in the milk, ricotta cheese and salt. Cook until heated through, stirring frequently. Spoon onto a heated serving platter. Top with the slivered ham; sprinkle with the freshly grated Parmesan cheese and freshly ground pepper. Yield: 8 servings.

# Apple-Stuffed Pork Tenderloin

Combine $^1/_2$ cup apple juice, butter and sage in a saucepan. Cook until heated through, stirring occasionally. Stir in the stuffing, apple and onion. Cut each tenderloin lengthwise not quite through; flatten. Sprinkle generously with salt and pepper. Spread the apple stuffing mixture over the cut side of 1 flattened tenderloin; top with the remaining tenderloin. Secure with skewers. Place in a shallow baking pan. Pour 1 cup apple juice over the tenderloins; top with the bacon. Roast at 350 degrees for $1^1/_2$ hours or until cooked through. Remove the skewers. Remove the tenderloins to a serving platter. Make gravy using the pan drippings if desired.
Yield: 6 to 8 servings.

$1^1/_2$ cups apple juice, divided
1     tablespoon butter
1     teaspoon sage
$^3/_4$   cup herb-seasoned stuffing
$^3/_4$   cup chopped unpeeled tart apple
$^1/_2$   cup chopped onion
2     (1-pound) whole pork tenderloins
     Salt and pepper to taste
4     slices bacon, cut into halves

# Grilled Pork Tenderloin with Prune-Onion Conserve

1/2 cup peanut oil
1/3 cup soy sauce
1/4 cup red wine vinegar
3 tablespoons lemon juice
2 tablespoons Worcestershire sauce
1 clove of garlic, crushed
1 tablespoon chopped fresh parsley
1 tablespoon dry mustard
1 1/2 teaspoons pepper
2 (3/4- to 1-pound) pork tenderloins
Prune-Onion Conserve

Combine the peanut oil, soy sauce, wine vinegar, lemon juice, Worcestershire sauce, garlic, parsley, dry mustard and pepper in a bowl and mix well. Pour over the pork tenderloins in a shallow dish, turning to coat. Marinate, covered, in the refrigerator for 4 hours or longer, turning occasionally. Reserve marinade. Grill 6 inches above hot (300 to 400 degrees) coals, basting occasionally with marinade, for 12 to 14 minutes or until cooked through, turning once. Serve with warm Prune-Onion Conserve.
Yield: 6 to 8 servings.

## Prune-Onion Conserve

1/2 cup chopped prunes
  Sherry
1/2 onion, thinly sliced
2 tablespoons unsalted butter
1 teaspoon tarragon
1/2 cup orange juice
1 teaspoon Dijon mustard
  Salt and pepper to taste

Plump the prunes in enough sherry to cover in a bowl for 30 minutes; drain. Sauté the onion in the butter in a saucepan until tender. Stir in the tarragon. Cook for 5 minutes longer, stirring frequently; do not brown onions. Add the prunes, orange juice, Dijon mustard, salt and pepper. Cook just until heated through, stirring constantly.
Yield: 6 to 8 servings.

# Jiffy Choucroute Garnie

*This Alsatian classic is an easy-to-assemble one-dish meal for hearty appetites. It is a great Oktoberfest meal. Serve with plenty of mustard and parslied new potatoes.*

Cook the bacon in a Dutch oven over low heat for 5 minutes or until most of the fat has been rendered. Stir in the onions and garlic. Reduce heat to low. Cook, covered, for 15 minutes or longer, stirring occasionally. Stir in the sauerkraut. Add the cumin seeds, salt, pepper, juniper berries, clove and bay leaf and mix well. Layer the sausage, frankfurters and pork chops over the sauerkraut mixture. Pour the white wine over the top. Bring to a boil. Place in a 350-degree oven. Bake, covered, for 50 minutes. Discard the bay leaf and whole clove. Spoon the sauerkraut mixture onto a large serving platter. Arrange the sausage, frankfurters and pork chops around the edge of the platter. Yield: 8 to 10 servings.

8   ounces sliced lean smoked bacon, cut into 1-inch strips
2   large onions, coarsely chopped
4   large cloves of garlic, crushed
4   pounds sauerkraut, drained
1   teaspoon cumin seeds
1   teaspoon salt
1   teaspoon pepper
8   juniper berries, lightly crushed
1   whole clove
1   bay leaf
1 1/2   pounds smoked Polish sausage
8   to 10 frankfurters or bratwurst
8   boneless smoked pork chops
3   cups Riesling or other white wine

# Chicken with Cilantro Pesto

4   boneless chicken breasts
    Juice of 1 large lemon
    Freshly ground pepper
2   cups packed cilantro leaves
³/₄  cup freshly grated Parmesan
    cheese
¹/₃  cup pine nuts
¹/₄  cup olive oil
2   tablespoons minced garlic
2   tablespoons fresh lime juice

Rinse the chicken and pat dry. Arrange in a shallow greased baking dish. Drizzle with the lemon juice; sprinkle with the pepper. Marinate, covered, in the refrigerator for 3 to 4 hours, turning occasionally. Process the cilantro, cheese, pine nuts, olive oil, garlic and lime juice in a food processor or blender until puréed or of pesto consistency. Bake the chicken at 400 degrees for 10 minutes. Spread 2 tablespoons of the pesto on top of each chicken breast. Cook for 10 minutes longer or until cooked through. Yield: 4 servings.

# Cajun Chicken Alfredo

9   ounces fettuccini
1   pound boneless skinless chicken
    breasts
1   clove of garlic, minced
6   tablespoons butter, divided
    Cajun seasoning to taste
¹/₄  cup Luzianne Cajun Chicken
    Coating Mix
2   cups half-and-half
³/₄  cup freshly grated Parmesan
    cheese

Cook the pasta using package directions. Drain and rinse in cold water. Rinse the chicken and pat dry. Cut into 1-inch pieces. Sauté the garlic in 2 tablespoons butter in a saucepan. Add the chicken. Cook until cooked through, stirring frequently. Sprinkle with Cajun seasoning if desired. Remove the chicken with a slotted spoon to a platter. Heat 4 tablespoons butter in the same saucepan until melted. Stir in the Coating Mix until blended. Add the half-and-half gradually and mix well. Cook until bubbly, stirring constantly. Add the cheese and mix well. Cook until thickened, stirring constantly. Stir in the chicken and pasta. Spoon onto a serving platter; sprinkle with Cajun seasoning. Serve immediately. May substitute flour for the Coating Mix. May add chopped vegetables to mixture. Yield: 4 servings.

# Davenport Chicken

Rinse the chicken and pat dry. Sprinkle with paprika, salt and pepper. Sauté the chicken in $1/4$ cup of the butter in a skillet until brown on all sides. Transfer the chicken with a slotted spoon to a 9x12-inch baking dish. Arrange the artichokes around the chicken. Add the remaining $1/4$ cup butter, mushrooms and tarragon to the same skillet. Sauté for 5 minutes. Add the flour gradually and mix well. Stir in the bouillon and sherry. Simmer for 5 minutes, stirring frequently. Pour over the chicken and artichokes. Bake, covered, at 375 degrees for 45 minutes. Yield: 4 servings.

4   *boneless skinless chicken breasts*
    *Paprika to taste*
    *Salt and pepper to taste*
$1/2$  *cup butter*
1   *(15-ounce) can artichoke hearts, drained*
4   *ounces fresh mushrooms, sliced*
    *Pinch of tarragon*
3   *tablespoons flour*
$1^1/2$ *cups chicken bouillon or stock*
$1/3$  *cup sherry*

# Forsyth Park Barbecued Chicken

Rinse the chicken and pat dry. Arrange in a nonreactive shallow dish. Combine $1^1/2$ cups sherry, soy sauce, 2 cloves of garlic and gingerroot in a bowl and mix well. Pour over the chicken, turning to coat. Marinate, covered, in the refrigerator for several hours to overnight, turning occasionally. Drain, discarding the marinade. Arrange in a shallow baking pan. Pour a mixture of 1 cup sherry, hoisin sauce, catsup, brown sugar and 1 clove of garlic over the chicken. Bake at 350 degrees for 20 minutes or until cooked through, basting occasionally and turning once. May grill over hot coals but do not baste while grilling. Yield: 12 servings.

4   *pounds boneless chicken breasts, split*
$1^1/2$ *cups dry sherry*
$1/2$  *cup low-sodium soy sauce*
2   *large cloves of garlic, minced*
2   *tablespoons minced fresh ginger*
1   *cup dry sherry*
$3/4$  *cup hoisin sauce*
$1/2$  *cup catsup*
$1/4$  *cup packed dark brown sugar*
1   *clove of garlic, minced*

# Pecan-Crusted Chicken

| | |
|---|---|
| 4 | (5- to 6-ounce) boneless chicken breasts |
| | Salt and pepper to taste |
| 1/2 | cup milk or half-and-half |
| 1 | egg |
| 1 | cup ground pecans |
| 1/4 | cup bread crumbs |
| 1/2 | cup flour |
| 4 | tablespoons vegetable oil |
| 1 | cup blackberry preserves |
| 1 | cup red wine |

*This recipe was contributed by The Olde Pink House.*

Rinse the chicken and pat dry. Sprinkle with salt and pepper. Combine the milk and egg in a bowl and mix well. Combine the pecans, bread crumbs and flour in a shallow dish and mix well. Dip the chicken in the milk mixture; coat with the pecan mixture. Sauté the chicken in the oil in a skillet until brown on all sides, turning occasionally. Transfer the chicken to a baking pan. Bake at 350 degrees for 8 to 10 minutes or until cooked through. Heat the preserves and wine in a saucepan, stirring occasionally. Serve with the chicken. Yield: 4 servings.

# Prosciutto-Stuffed Chicken Breasts with Béarnaise Sauce

Rinse the chicken and pat dry. Flatten the chicken breasts 1/4 inch thick between sheets of waxed paper with a rolling pin. Place 1 slice of prosciutto on each chicken breast. Combine the olive oil, 2 tablespoons parsley, tarragon, peppercorns, garlic, salt and pepper in a bowl and mix well. Spoon 1 tablespoon of the herb mixture on each prosciutto slice. Roll the chicken breasts to enclose the filling; secure each with 2 wooden picks. Place seam side down in a baking dish. Spoon the remaining herb mixture over the chicken. Bake at 350 degrees for 15 minutes. Pour the hot chicken stock over the chicken. Bake for 20 to 25 minutes longer or until cooked through, basting frequently. Add 1 tablespoon parsley to the baking dish and mix well. Remove the wooden picks from the chicken breasts and cut into medallions. Arrange the medallions on a serving platter; drizzle with the Béarnaise Sauce. Yield: 4 servings.

| 4 | chicken breasts, cut into halves, boned, skinned |
| 4 | slices prosciutto |
| 1/4 | cup olive oil |
| 3 | tablespoons chopped fresh parsley, divided |
| 2 | tablespoons chopped fresh tarragon, or 1 tablespoon dried tarragon |
| 1 | tablespoon peppercorns, crushed |
| 1 | clove of garlic, chopped |
| | Salt and pepper to taste |
| 1/2 | cup chicken stock, heated |
| | Béarnaise Sauce |

## Béarnaise Sauce

Heat 1 tablespoon of the butter in a saucepan until melted. Stir in the shallots, wine vinegar, tarragon, chervil, salt and peppercorns. Cook until reduced to 2 teaspoons, stirring constantly. Clarify the remaining butter. Combine the tarragon mixture and egg yolks in a stainless steel bowl. Place over a pan of hot water. Whisk until the mixture is of the consistency of whipping cream. Remove from heat. Blend in the clarified butter. Cover to keep warm. The sauce should have the consistency of mustard. Yield: 4 servings.

| 1 | cup unsalted butter |
| 3 | medium shallots, finely chopped |
| 3 | tablespoons white wine vinegar |
| 2 | sprigs of tarragon |
| 1/4 | teaspoon chopped fresh chervil |
| | Salt to taste |
| | Pinch of crushed peppercorns |
| 4 | egg yolks |

# Bay Street Chicken and Shrimp

| | |
|---|---|
| 1 | cup chopped green onions |
| 1 | teaspoon dried tarragon, divided |
| 1/4 | cup butter |
| 2 | cups thickly sliced mushrooms |
| 2 | cups chopped cooked chicken breast |
| 1 | cup chopped red bell pepper |
| 1/2 | cup dry white wine |
| 2 | cups deveined peeled shrimp |
| 1/2 | cup butter |
| 2 | tablespoons flour |
| 2 | cups half-and-half |
| 1/4 | cup dry white wine |
| | Salt and pepper to taste |

Sauté the green onions and 1/2 teaspoon tarragon in 1/4 cup butter in a skillet for 5 minutes. Add the mushrooms, chicken, red pepper and 1/2 cup white wine and mix well. Bring to a simmer, stirring constantly. Add the shrimp and 1/2 teaspoon tarragon and mix well. Sauté until the shrimp turn pink, stirring frequently. Remove from heat. Heat 1/2 cup butter in a saucepan until melted. Whisk in the flour until blended. Add the half-and-half. Cook until thickened, stirring constantly. Stir in 1/4 cup white wine, salt and pepper; do not boil. Bring the shrimp mixture to a simmer, stirring frequently. Add the sauce and mix well. Simmer just until heated through, stirring constantly. Serve over white or yellow rice. Yield: 6 to 8 servings.

# Stir-Fry Chicken with Vidalia Onion

| | |
|---|---|
| 4 | boneless skinless chicken breasts |
| 1/4 | cup soy sauce |
| 1 | tablespoon dry white wine |
| 2 | tablespoons cornstarch |
| 1 | teaspoon sugar |
| 1/8 | teaspoon garlic powder |
| 7 | tablespoons peanut oil |
| 1/4 | cup chicken broth |
| 1 | red bell pepper, chopped |
| 1 | green bell pepper, chopped |
| 1 | large Vidalia onion, coarsely chopped |
| 1 1/4 | cups lightly salted cashews |

Rinse the chicken and pat dry. Cut into bite-size pieces. Place in a shallow dish. Combine the soy sauce and white wine in a bowl and mix well. Stir in the cornstarch, sugar and garlic powder. Pour over the chicken, stirring to mix. Marinate, covered, in the refrigerator for 2 hours, stirring occasionally. Heat 5 tablespoons of the peanut oil and the broth in a wok or skillet until hot. Add the undrained chicken mixture. Stir-fry for 5 minutes or until the chicken is cooked through. Remove the chicken mixture to a bowl. Heat the remaining 2 tablespoons of peanut oil in the wok or skillet. Add the red pepper, green pepper and onion. Stir-fry for 3 minutes. Add the chicken mixture and cashews and mix well. Serve immediately with hot cooked rice. Yield: 6 servings.

# Chicken Potpie

*Cook the chicken one day in advance and it will be easier to remove from the bone, as well as save time the day of preparation.*

Rinse the chicken. Combine the chicken with enough water to cover in a stockpot. Simmer for 1 hour or until cooked through. Drain, reserving 1 cup of the broth. Let the chicken stand until cool. Chop the chicken, discarding the skin and bones. Sauté the carrots, onion, celery and garlic in the butter in a saucepan until tender. Stir in the peas. Add the flour, stirring until mixed. Add the reserved chicken broth and half-and-half gradually and mix well. Cook over medium-low heat until thickened, stirring constantly. Stir in the chicken. Season with salt and pepper. Press one of the pastries over the bottom and up the sides of a 2-quart baking dish. Spoon the chicken mixture into the baking dish. Top with the remaining pastry, sealing edges and cutting vents. Bake at 375 degrees for 40 minutes or until light brown and bubbly. Yield: 6 to 8 servings.

1   chicken
1¹/2 cups peeled sliced carrots
1   medium to large onion, chopped
3   ribs celery, chopped
1   large clove of garlic, crushed
¹/4 cup butter
1   (10-ounce) package frozen peas
4   tablespoons (heaping) flour
1   cup half-and-half
    Salt and pepper to taste
2   all ready pie pastries

# Grilled Chicken with Wine Marinade

| 1 | chicken, cut up |
| 1 | cup dry white wine |
| 3/4 | cup olive oil |
| 1/4 | cup tarragon vinegar |
| 3 | cloves of garlic, minced |
| 1 | tablespoon fresh oregano |
| 1 | tablespoon fresh basil |
| 2 | teaspoons salt |
| 1 | teaspoon pepper |

Rinse the chicken and pat dry. Arrange in a single layer in a 9x13-inch dish. Combine the white wine, olive oil, tarragon vinegar, garlic, oregano, basil, salt and pepper in a saucepan. Cook over medium heat for 5 minutes, stirring occasionally. Remove from heat. Let stand until cool. Pour 1/2 of the marinade over the chicken, turning to coat. Reserve the remaining marinade for basting. Marinate, covered, in the refrigerator overnight, turning occasionally. Drain, discarding the marinade. Microwave the reserved marinade in a microwave-safe dish until hot. Arrange the chicken skin side down on a grill rack 4 to 6 inches above the hot coals. Grill for 6 to 8 minutes; turn and baste with the hot reserved marinade. Grill for 20 minutes longer or until the juices run clear when the thigh is pricked with a fork, basting occasionally with the hot reserved marinade. Yield: 4 servings.

# Cornish Hens with Stilton Sauce

| 4 | Cornish game hens |
|  | Salt and pepper to taste |
| 1/2 | cup unsalted butter |
| 8 | ounces fresh mushrooms, sliced |
| 1/4 | cup brandy |
| 1 1/4 | cups half-and-half |
| 4 | ounces Stilton cheese, crumbled |
|  | Parsley (optional) |

Rinse the game hens and pat dry. Sprinkle inside and outside with salt and pepper. Arrange in a baking pan. Dot the game hens with 1/4 cup of the butter. Roast at 375 degrees for 50 to 55 minutes or until cooked through. Sauté the mushrooms in the remaining 1/4 cup butter in a skillet for 5 minutes; reduce heat. Stir in the brandy. Simmer for 15 minutes, stirring frequently; increase heat. Stir in the half-and-half. Cook for 12 to 15 minutes or until of the desired consistency, stirring constantly. Stir in the cheese. Cook until thickened, stirring constantly. Arrange the game hens on a serving platter. Cover with 1/2 of the sauce. Garnish with sprigs of fresh parsley. Serve with the remaining sauce. Yield: 4 servings.

# Monterey Cornish Hens

Rinse the game hens and pat dry. Make several slits in the skin; split each hen into halves. Mix the lime juice, 1 teaspoon chili powder, salt and pepper in a bowl. Rub mixture over the game hens. Let stand for 15 minutes. Process the yogurt, onion, garlic, gingerroot, cumin seeds, sugar, turmeric and 1/2 teaspoon chili powder in a blender until puréed. Pour over the game hens in a bowl, turning to coat. Marinate, covered, in the refrigerator for 8 hours or longer, turning occasionally. Drain, reserving the marinade. Arrange the game hens skin side up on a rack in a roasting pan. Spoon the reserved marinade over the game hens. Bake at 400 degrees, basting frequently, for 45 to 60 minutes or until the juices run clear when the thigh is pricked with a fork. Remove the skin from the game hens. Arrange on a serving platter. Garnish with lime wedges and sprigs of fresh cilantro or parsley. Yield: 6 servings.

3    *(1-pound) Cornish game hens*
3    *tablespoons fresh lime juice*
1    *teaspoon chili powder, or to taste*
1/2  *teaspoon salt (optional)*
     *Freshly ground pepper to taste*
1    *cup plain nonfat yogurt*
1    *small onion, coarsely chopped*
3    *cloves of garlic*
1    *(1-inch) piece fresh ginger,*
     *coarsely chopped*
1    *teaspoon cumin seeds*
1    *teaspoon sugar*
1/2  *teaspoon turmeric*
1/2  *teaspoon chili powder, or to taste*

# Grilled Doves

Rinse the doves and pat dry. Sprinkle with salt and pepper. Arrange in a shallow dish. Pour the salad dressing over the doves, turning to coat. Marinate, covered, in the refrigerator for 2 to 6 hours, turning occasionally. Drain, discarding the marinade. Arrange the doves on a grill rack. Lay a bacon slice on top of each dove. Grill, covered, over hot coals for 10 to 12 minutes or until slightly pink in middle. Yield: 2 to 4 servings.

10   *to 12 doves*
     *Salt and pepper to taste*
     *Italian salad dressing*
     *Bacon slices*

# Duck with Blackberry Sauce

8   boneless duck breasts
    Salt and pepper to taste
2   tablespoons butter
    Blackberry Sauce

*Wild or domestic ducks may be used. Wrap wild ducks with a slice of bacon. Leave the skin on domestic ducks.*

Rinse the duck and pat dry. Sprinkle with salt and pepper. Cut a few slits in the fat of domestic duck. Heat the butter in a heavy ovenproof skillet over high heat until melted. Arrange the duck skin side down in the prepared skillet. Sear the duck for 5 minutes; turn. Sear for 3 minutes longer. Bake at 400 degrees for 5 minutes. Arrange the duck on a serving platter. Drizzle with the warm Blackberry Sauce. Garnish with blackberries. Yield: 8 servings.

## Blackberry Sauce

2       tablespoons butter
3       tablespoons sugar
$^1/_3$   cup dry white wine
$^1/_3$   cup orange juice
2       tablespoons raspberry vinegar
$1^1/_4$ cups frozen blackberries, thawed
$1^1/_4$ cups beef broth
$^1/_2$   cup canned low-sodium chicken broth
2       tablespoons brandy
1       tablespoon maple syrup

Heat the butter in a heavy nonstick skillet until melted. Stir in the sugar. Cook until the sugar dissolves and the mixture is deep amber in color, stirring constantly. Add the white wine, orange juice and raspberry vinegar and mix well. Bring to a boil, stirring constantly until blended. Stir in the blackberries, beef broth and chicken broth. Boil until thickened and mixture is reduced to 1 cup, stirring occasionally. Strain through a sieve, pressing berries with back of a spoon. Stir in the brandy and maple syrup. Yield: 8 servings.

# Seared Quail with Brandied Boar Bacon and Peppercorn Cream

*This recipe was contributed by 45 South.*

For the quail, rinse the quail and pat dry. Season with salt and pepper. Heat a heavy skillet until hot. Add the duck fat. Sear the quail skin side down in the hot skillet until brown and crisp; turn. Remove from heat. Let stand for 30 seconds. Remove the birds to a serving platter with a slotted spoon, reserving the pan drippings. For the sauce, add the bacon and shallot to the reserved pan drippings. Sauté until the shallot is tender. Deglaze the skillet with the brandy. Stir in the duck stock. Cook until reduced by 2/3, stirring constantly. Add the whipping cream and mix well. Cook until reduced by 1/2, stirring constantly. Stir in the peppercorns. Pour the sauce over the birds. Yield: 4 servings.

4   partially deboned (European-Style) quail
    Kosher salt and freshly ground pepper to taste
1   teaspoon rendered duck fat
2   ounces rendered boar bacon, chopped
2   tablespoons chopped shallot
1/4 cup brandy
3/4 cup duck stock
1/2 cup whipping cream
1   teaspoon green peppercorns

# Turkey Breast Supreme

1    medium onion, sliced
2    cloves of garlic
1    (5- to 6-pound) turkey breast
      Olive oil
1    teaspoon salt
1    teaspoon paprika
1    teaspoon dried sage
1/2  teaspoon pepper
1/4  cup white wine

*This is a great recipe to cook while away from the house. Before beginning, read the entire recipe. Cooking time is important.*

Line a 9x13-inch baking pan with foil, leaving enough overhang to enclose the turkey. Arrange the onion and garlic in the prepared pan. Rinse the turkey and pat dry. Brush all sides of the turkey with olive oil. Place in the prepared pan. Combine the salt, paprika, sage and pepper in a bowl and mix well. Sprinkle over the turkey. Bake, uncovered, at 350 degrees for 30 minutes. Pour the white wine over the turkey; seal with foil. Reduce the oven temperature to 200 degrees. Bake a 5-pound turkey for 7 hours and bake a 6-pound turkey for 8 hours. Yield: 10 to 12 servings.

# Cobblestone Crab and Shrimp

Chop the artichoke leaves; cut the bottoms into quarters. Heat the butter in a saucepan until melted. Stir in the flour. Cook for 5 minutes, stirring frequently. Add the green onions and onion and mix well. Cook for 2 minutes; do not brown. Stir in the parsley. Add the whipping cream and mix well. Stir in the white wine, salt, black pepper and cayenne. Bring to a simmer, stirring constantly. Add the cheese and mix well. Remove from heat and cover. Let stand until cool. Stir in the artichoke leaves and lemon juice. Layer the shrimp, crab meat, mushrooms, quartered artichoke bottoms and cheese sauce $^1/_2$ at a time in a 3-quart baking dish. May chill, covered, at this point until just before baking. Bake, uncovered, at 350 degrees for 30 to 45 minutes or until bubbly. Serve with fresh bread and a salad.
Yield: 10 to 12 servings.

1   (16-ounce) can artichokes, drained
$^1/_2$   cup butter
$^1/_2$   cup flour
$^1/_2$   cup chopped green onions
$^1/_4$   cup grated white onion
2   tablespoons chopped fresh parsley
2   cups whipping cream
1   cup dry white wine
$2^1/_2$ teaspoons salt
$^1/_2$   teaspoon black pepper
$^1/_4$   teaspoon cayenne
$2^1/_2$ ounces Swiss cheese, shredded
2   tablespoons lemon juice
2   pounds medium shrimp, cooked, peeled
1   pound lump or claw crab meat
8   ounces fresh mushroom caps, thickly sliced

# Crab Cakes Savannah

1    pound lump crab meat, flaked
1    egg, beaten
1    tablespoon mayonnaise
2    teaspoons lemon juice
1    teaspoon yellow mustard
1    teaspoon Dijonnaise
    Several drops of Worcestershire
    sauce
    Old Bay seasoning to taste
    Black pepper to taste
    Cayenne to taste
8    to 10 saltine crackers, crushed
8    to 10 saltine crackers, finely
    crushed
1/4   cup butter
3    tablespoons vegetable oil

Combine the crab meat, egg, mayonnaise, lemon juice, yellow mustard, Dijonnaise, Worcestershire sauce, Old Bay seasoning, black pepper and cayenne in a bowl and mix gently. Stir in the crushed crackers. Shape into eight 1/2-inch-thick patties. Coat with the finely crushed crackers. Arrange in a dish. Chill or freeze the crab cakes until firm. Heat the butter and oil in a skillet until hot. Sauté the crab cakes in the butter mixture until brown on both sides; drain. Yield: 8 servings.

# Crab Pie

1    (unbaked) 9-inch deep-dish
    pie shell
1/2   cup mayonnaise
1/2   cup milk
1/4   cup chopped green onions
2    eggs, beaten
2    tablespoons flour
1/2   teaspoon salt
1    pound crab meat, flaked
8    slices Swiss cheese, torn into
    bite-size pieces

Bake the pie shell at 350 degrees just until the shell begins to brown. Combine the mayonnaise, milk, green onions, eggs, flour and salt in a bowl and mix well. Fold in the crab meat and cheese. Spoon into the baked pie shell. Bake at 350 degrees for 40 to 50 minutes or until brown. Yield: 6 servings.

# Oysters and Spinach

Cook the spinach using package directions, omitting the salt; drain. Squeeze the moisture from the spinach. Spread in a lightly greased 1-quart baking dish. Layer the oysters over the spinach. Sprinkle with the cheese, garlic powder and pepper. Top with the bacon. Drizzle with a mixture of the butter and lemon juice. Bake at 450 degrees for 8 to 10 minutes or until the edges of the oysters curl. Yield: 4 servings.

1   (10-ounce) package frozen chopped spinach
1/2   pint oysters, drained
1/4   cup grated Parmesan cheese
1/8   teaspoon garlic powder
1/8   teaspoon pepper
5   slices crisp-fried bacon, crumbled
2   tablespoons melted butter or margarine
1   tablespoon lemon juice

# Oysters with Creamed Corn

Combine the cracker crumbs and butter in a bowl and mix well. Combine the corn, whipping cream, salt and pepper in a bowl and mix well. Layer 1/2 of the cracker crumb mixture, the corn mixture, the oysters and the remaining cracker crumb mixture in a deep baking dish. Bake at 375 degrees for 45 minutes. Yield: 8 servings.

3   cups cracker crumbs
1/2   cup melted butter
4   cups canned cream-style corn or cooked fresh cream corn
1/2   cup whipping cream or half-and-half
1   teaspoon salt
1   teaspoon pepper
1   pint select oysters, drained

# Fish Fillets with Pasta

| | |
|---|---|
| 2 | pounds cod or trout fillets |
| | Salt and freshly ground pepper |
| | to taste |
| 8 | ounces slab bacon, sliced |
| 5 | medium onions, coarsely |
| | chopped |
| 4 | large or 6 medium tomatoes, |
| | peeled, chopped |
| 1 | tablespoon fresh lime juice |
| 1 | teaspoon sugar |
| 3 | cloves of garlic, minced |
| | Hot cooked pasta |

Rinse the fillets and pat dry. Season with salt and pepper. Cook the bacon in a skillet over medium-high heat for 5 minutes or until partially cooked; the bacon will be soft and fat will be translucent. Remove from heat. Remove the bacon to a platter, reserving the pan drippings. Arrange $1/2$ of the bacon in the bottom of a 9x13-inch baking pan. Arrange the fillets over the bacon. Top with the remaining bacon. Bake at 350 degrees for 20 to 25 minutes or until the fish flakes easily. Sauté the onions in the reserved pan drippings in the skillet over medium-high heat for 5 minutes. Stir in the tomatoes, lime juice, sugar and garlic. Cook for 25 minutes or until thickened and of sauce consistency. Season to taste. Pour over the fish. Serve immediately over hot cooked pasta. Yield: 6 to 8 servings.

# Oven-Fried Grouper

| | |
|---|---|
| 2 | pounds grouper fillets |
| 1 | egg, beaten |
| $1/2$ | cup Italian-seasoned bread |
| | crumbs |
| $1/4$ | cup melted margarine |
| 2 | tablespoons lemon juice |

*Catfish and snapper are good alternatives to the grouper.*

Dip the fillets in the egg; coat with the bread crumbs. Arrange the fish in a single layer in a greased shallow baking pan. Drizzle with a mixture of the margarine and lemon juice. Bake at 450 degrees for 15 to 18 minutes or until the fish flakes easily. Yield: 6 to 8 servings.

# Pan-Fried Pompano with Sautéed Spinach with Morels and Saffron Butter Sauce

*This recipe was contributed by 45 South.*

Sprinkle the fillets with the salt and pepper. Heat 2 tablespoons of the olive oil and 2 tablespoons of the butter in a skillet until the butter is golden brown. Add 2 of the fillets. Sauté for 45 to 60 seconds per side. Transfer the fillets to a platter. Wipe out the skillet and repeat the process with the remaining olive oil, butter and fillets. Arrange 2 fillets and the Sautéed Spinach with Morels on each of 4 dinner plates. Drizzle the Saffron Butter Sauce over the fillets. Yield: 4 servings.

8    (3- to 4-ounce) pompano fillets, skinned
     Kosher salt and freshly cracked pepper to taste
1/2  cup olive oil
1/2  cup unsalted butter
     Sautéed Spinach with Morels
     Saffron Butter Sauce

## Sautéed Spinach with Morels

Sauté the shallots and morels in 1/3 of the butter in a skillet until tender. Sauté the spinach with the remaining butter in a separate skillet. Squeeze excess moisture from the spinach. Stir the spinach into the shallot mixture. Season with salt and white pepper. Yield: 4 servings.

4    tablespoons minced shallots
1    ounce dried morels, rehydrated, julienned
1/4  cup unsalted butter
12   ounces fresh spinach leaves, trimmed
     Kosher salt and white pepper to taste

## Saffron Butter Sauce

Combine the white wine, shallots and saffron in a saucepan. Cook over medium heat until reduced by 3/4, stirring constantly; reduce heat. Add the butter gradually, whisking carefully after each addition. Season with salt and white pepper. Yield: 4 servings.

1/2  cup dry white wine
2    tablespoons minced shallots
1    pinch of Spanish saffron
3/4  cup unsalted butter, cut into 1/2-inch cubes
     Kosher salt and white pepper to taste

# Baked Red Snapper with
# Crispy Herbed Shrimp Topping

4   (1½ to 2 pounds) red snapper
    fillets with skin

**Marinade**
½   cup dry white wine
½   cup olive oil
¼   cup fresh lemon juice
1   clove of garlic, minced
    Salt and pepper to taste

8   ounces shrimp, cooked, peeled,
    chopped
1   cup cracker crumbs
¼   cup mayonnaise
¼   cup minced onion
¼   cup minced fresh parsley leaves
⅓   cup freshly grated Parmesan
    cheese
1   tablespoon drained capers,
    finely chopped
¼   teaspoon dried basil
¼   teaspoon dried tarragon
1   clove of garlic, minced

Arrange the fillets skin side up in a single layer in a 9x13-inch baking dish. Combine the white wine, olive oil, lemon juice, 1 clove of garlic, salt and pepper in a bowl and mix well. Reserve ¼ cup of the marinade. Pour the remaining marinade over the fillets. Marinate, covered, in the refrigerator for 3 hours, turning every hour. *For the shrimp mixture,* combine the shrimp, cracker crumbs, mayonnaise, onion, parsley leaves, cheese, capers, basil, tarragon, 1 clove of garlic, the reserved marinade, salt and pepper in a bowl and mix well. Bake the fillets skin side down in the marinade at 400 degrees for 10 minutes. Top with the shrimp mixture. Bake for 5 minutes longer. Broil for 5 minutes or until golden brown and crisp.
Yield: 4 servings.

# Grilled Salmon over Mashed Potatoes with Butter Beans

*Tuna or swordfish works well too. Simple to prepare. Serve with a chilled light dry white wine and conclude with a fresh fruit dessert.*

Remove skin from the salmon. Store, covered, in the refrigerator until time to grill. Combine the potatoes and broth in a saucepan, adding water if needed to cover. Cook over medium heat for 20 minutes or until tender; drain. Add the margarine, mashing to mix. Blend in the milk gradually. Add salt and white pepper. Cover partially to keep warm. May be prepared 1 hour in advance and kept at room temperature. Do not store in the refrigerator for more than 1 hour after the potatoes have cooled. Bring 2 cups lightly salted water to a boil in a saucepan. Add the butter beans. Cook for 20 to 25 minutes or until done to taste. Remove from heat. Let stand until cool. Store in the refrigerator if not using within 1 hour. Heat the grill 30 minutes before ready to serve. Spray the salmon on both sides with nonstick cooking spray. Remove the hot grill racks with heavy tongs. Spray with nonstick cooking spray. Return the grill racks to the grill. Place the fillets on the racks. Grill over medium-low heat for 7 minutes; turn. Grill for 5 minutes longer or until the salmon flakes easily. Reheat the potatoes and butter beans. Place a scoop of the potatoes in the center of each of 4 dinner plates. Surround each serving of potatoes with 1/2 cup drained butter beans. Arrange the salmon in the center of the potatoes. Drizzle the beans with a mixture of the butter, lemon juice and 1 or 2 drops of water. Garnish with lemon slices and/or fresh dillweed or parsley. Yield: 4 servings.

4   (5- to 6-ounce) salmon fillets
5   medium white russet potatoes or other variety, peeled, sliced
2   cups canned chicken broth or stock
4   to 5 tablespoons margarine, softened (optional)
1/2   to 3/4 cup milk or half-and-half, heated
    Salt and white pepper to taste
2   cups water
2   cups fresh or frozen baby butter beans
1/4   cup melted butter
1   tablespoon lemon juice
1   or 2 drops of water
    Lemon slices, fresh dill stems or parsley (optional)

# Poached Salmon with Basil Cream Sauce

4   peppercorns
1   bay leaf
4   salmon steaks, 1 to
     1¹/₂ inches thick
     Basil Cream Sauce

Pour water to a depth of 1 inch in a medium skillet. Add the peppercorns. Bring to a boil. Add the bay leaf and salmon; reduce heat. Simmer, covered, for 5 minutes or until the salmon flakes easily; do not overcook. Arrange the salmon steaks on a serving platter. Serve with Basil Cream Sauce.
Yield: 4 servings.

# Basil Cream Sauce

¹/₂  cup plain yogurt
¹/₂  cup mayonnaise
1    tablespoon whipping cream
1    green onion, chopped
2    tablespoons (heaping) chopped
     fresh parsley
2    tablespoons (heaping) chopped
     fresh basil
     Salt and pepper to taste

Combine the yogurt, mayonnaise, whipping cream, green onion, parsley, basil, salt and pepper in a bowl and mix well. Chill, covered, unless serving immediately. Yield: 1¹/₄ cups.

# Grilled Tuna

Arrange the steaks in a shallow dish. Pour the salad dressing over the steaks, turning to coat. Marinate in the refrigerator for 1 to 2 hours, turning occasionally; do not marinate longer than 2 hours. Drain, reserving the marinade. Preheat the grill on high; reduce heat to medium. Grill the tuna steaks over medium-hot coals for 10 minutes, turning and basting with the reserved marinade occasionally. Arrange the onion slices on the tuna. Grill for 5 minutes longer or until the tuna flakes easily. Arrange on a serving platter; drizzle with the lemon juice. Sprinkle with the seasoned salt. Serve with the lemon slices.  Yield: 4 servings.

4   tuna steaks, 1/2 inch thick
1 1/2 cups fat-free Italian salad
     dressing
     Vidalia onion slices
     Juice of 1 lemon
1   tablespoon seasoned salt
1   to 2 lemons, sliced

# Tuna or Dolphin Macadamia

Sprinkle the fillets with salt and pepper. Sear on both sides in the olive oil in a skillet. Transfer the fillets with a slotted spoon to a baking pan, reserving the pan drippings. Bake at 350 degrees until the fish flakes easily. Sauté the pineapple and garlic in the reserved pan drippings in the skillet. Add the white wine and pineapple juice and mix well. Cook until reduced by 1/2, stirring constantly. Stir in the whipping cream. Cook until slightly reduced, stirring constantly. Stir in a mixture of the cornstarch and a small amount of water. Cook until thickened, stirring constantly. Stir in the macadamia nuts and cilantro. Season with salt and pepper. Arrange the fillets on a serving platter; top with the sauce. Serve with herbed rice, grilled or seared pineapple slices and broccoli sautéed in butter. Yield: 6 servings.

6   tuna or dolphin fillets
     Salt and pepper to taste
2   tablespoons olive oil
1   cup chopped pineapple
1   teaspoon minced garlic
1   cup white wine
1   cup pineapple juice
1   cup whipping cream
1   to 2 tablespoons cornstarch
1   cup chopped macadamia nuts,
     toasted
1   teaspoon minced fresh cilantro

# Scallops and Shrimp Mornay

1/4 cup butter
1/4 cup flour
2 cups milk
2 tablespoons sherry
Salt to taste
8 ounces scallops
8 ounces shrimp, peeled
2 tablespoons butter
Seasoned salt to taste
1/4 cup finely chopped green onions
1/4 cup finely chopped fresh parsley
4 puff pastry shells, baked

*Very attractive to serve for a spring luncheon or dinner party.*

Heat 1/4 cup butter in a saucepan until melted. Add the flour, stirring until blended. Add the milk gradually, stirring constantly. Cook until of the consistency of a thick cream sauce, stirring constantly. Whisk in the sherry. Season with salt. Remove from heat. Sauté the scallops and shrimp in 2 tablespoons butter in a skillet until the shrimp turn pink and the scallops are tender. Sprinkle with seasoned salt. Stir the shrimp mixture, green onions and parsley into the cream sauce. Cook just until heated through, stirring frequently. Arrange the pastry shells on individual dinner plates. Spoon the Scallops and Shrimp Mornay into the shells. Yield: 4 servings.

# Scallop Kabobs with Peach Salsa

Thread the zucchini, yellow squash, scallops, artichokes and onions alternately onto skewers until all the ingredients are used. Brush with the olive oil; drizzle with lime juice. Grill over hot coals for 8 minutes or until the scallops are tender, turning occasionally. Serve with Peach Salsa. Yield: 8 servings.

3  medium zucchini, cut into
   *1/2-inch slices*
3  yellow squash, cut into
   *1/2-inch slices*
5  dozen sea scallops
5  jars artichoke heart quarters,
   drained
3  large Vidalia onions, cut into
   quarters
1/2  cup virgin olive oil
   Juice of 2 limes
   Peach Salsa

# Peach Salsa

Combine the bell pepper, cucumber, green onions and jalapeño in a food processor container. Mix by pulsing several times, being careful not to chop too finely. Pour into a bowl. Stir in the honey, lime juice and cilantro. Place the peaches in the food processor container. Pulse several times. Stir the peaches into the salsa mixture. Chill, covered, for several hours. Yield: 2 to 3 cups.

1  cup coarsely chopped red, yellow
   and/or green bell pepper
1/4  cup coarsely chopped seeded
   peeled cucumber
1/4  cup chopped green onions, white
   part only
1  jalapeño (or more), coarsely
   chopped
2  tablespoons honey
2  tablespoons lime juice
1  to 2 tablespoons chopped fresh
   cilantro
2  cups coarsely chopped peeled
   peaches

# Baked Shrimp with Spinach Noodles

| | |
|---|---|
| 8 | ounces spinach noodles or fettuccini |
| 2 | pounds shrimp, peeled, deveined |
| 1/4 | cup butter |
| 1 | cup sour cream |
| 1 | cup mayonnaise |
| 1 | (10-ounce) can cream of mushroom soup |
| 1/4 | cup dry sherry |
| 1 | tablespoon chopped fresh chives |
| 1 | teaspoon Dijon mustard |
| 1 | cup shredded sharp Cheddar cheese, grated |

Cook the noodles using package directions, cutting the cooking time in half; drain. Arrange the noodles in a large buttered baking dish. Sauté the shrimp in 1/4 cup butter in a saucepan for 5 minutes or until the shrimp turn pink. Spoon the shrimp and pan drippings over the noodles. Combine the sour cream, mayonnaise, soup, sherry, chives and Dijon mustard in a bowl and mix well. Pour over the shrimp; sprinkle with the cheese. Bake at 350 degrees for 30 minutes or until bubbly. May be prepared 1 day in advance, stored in the refrigerator overnight and baked just before serving. Yield: 8 servings.

# Tybee Fried Shrimp

*The sour cream destroys the iodine in the shrimp,*
*giving them a sweet taste.*

Combine the shrimp and sour cream in a bowl
and mix well. Let stand for 30 minutes. Coat the
shrimp with the flour. Heat the oil in a deep fryer
to 350 degrees. Deep-fry the shrimp by batches
in the hot oil for 5 minutes or until golden brown;
drain. Sprinkle with salt. If the oil begins to burn,
lower the heat and add 1 or 2 slices of bacon to
the oil. Yield: 4 servings.

1   pound shrimp, peeled, deveined
1/2  cup sour cream
1   cup flour
    Vegetable oil for deep-frying
    Salt to taste
1   to 2 slices bacon (optional)

# Savannah Shrimp Curry

Sauté the onion and celery in the margarine in a
saucepan until tender. Stir in the boiling water and
bouillon cube. Sprinkle in the flour, curry powder,
salt and ginger powder and mix well. Add the milk
and lemon juice and mix well. Simmer until
thickened, stirring constantly. Stir in the shrimp
and cayenne. Simmer just until heated through,
stirring frequently. Serve over hot rice.
Yield: 4 to 6 servings.

1      medium onion, minced
1      cup minced celery
5      tablespoons margarine
1      cup boiling water
1      chicken bouillon cube
6      tablespoons flour
1      to 2 tablespoons curry powder
1 1/4  teaspoons salt
1/4    teaspoon ginger powder
2      cups milk
1      teaspoon lemon juice
2      pounds shrimp, peeled, cooked
       Cayenne to taste

# Shrimp Hollandaise

2   pounds shrimp, peeled, deveined
1   pound mushrooms, sliced
1   cup butter
1¹/2 cups mayonnaise
1   onion, grated
2   tablespoons horseradish
¹/2  teaspoon dry mustard
¹/2  teaspoon salt
¹/2  teaspoon hot vinegar
    Hot cooked rice

Sauté the shrimp and mushrooms in ¹/2 cup of the butter in a skillet until the shrimp turn pink. Remove the shrimp and mushrooms with a slotted spoon to a bowl. Cover to keep warm. Cook the pan drippings until thickened, stirring constantly. Whisk in the remaining ¹/2 cup butter, mayonnaise, onion, horseradish, dry mustard, salt and hot vinegar. Cook just until heated through, stirring constantly. Remove from heat. Spoon the rice onto a serving platter; top with the shrimp mixture; top with the hollandaise sauce. Yield: 6 servings.

# Shrimp Wilmington

8   ounces fresh mushrooms
¹/4  cup butter
1   (10-ounce) can shrimp soup
1   cup sour cream
1   teaspoon soy sauce
¹/4  teaspoon pepper
1¹/2 pounds shrimp, peeled, cooked
    Sherry to taste

Sauté the mushrooms in the butter in a saucepan until wilted but still white. Stir in the soup, sour cream, soy sauce and pepper. Cook until smooth and bubbly, stirring constantly. Fold in the shrimp. Stir in the sherry. Serve over hot cooked rice or spoon over a croissant. Yield: 6 servings.

# Shrimp and Feta Pizzas

Combine the lukewarm water, yeast and sugar in a bowl and mix well. Let stand for 5 minutes or until foamy. Stir in the olive oil and sea salt. Add the bread flour gradually, mixing until the dough forms a ball. Knead on a lightly floured surface for 4 to 5 minutes until satiny but firm. May add additional flour if needed for desired consistency. Place in a bowl; cover tightly with a damp tea towel. Place in a cool oven. Let rise for 2 to 3 hours or until doubled or tripled in bulk. (May freeze the dough at this point. Punch the dough down, brush with olive oil, wrap in plastic wrap and place in a plastic freezer container.) *To prepare*, divide the dough into 2 equal portions. Roll each portion on a lightly floured surface to fit a pizza pan. Sprinkle each pizza pan with cornmeal. Fit the dough into the prepared pizza pans. Spread each prepared layer with 1/2 of the tomato paste; sprinkle with oregano and basil. Top each with 1/2 of the red pepper, 1/2 of the yellow pepper, 1/2 of the mushrooms, 1/2 of the feta cheese, 1/2 of the shrimp, 1/2 of the Parmesan cheese and 1/2 of the mozzarella cheese. Bake at 450 degrees for 10 minutes or until brown and bubbly.
Yield: 2 pizzas.

**Crust**

| | |
|---|---|
| 1 1/3 | cups lukewarm water |
| 1 | teaspoon fast-rising dry yeast |
| 1 | teaspoon sugar |
| 2 | tablespoons extra-virgin olive oil |
| 1 | teaspoon sea salt |
| 3 3/4 | cups bread flour |

| | |
|---|---|
| | Yellow cornmeal |
| 1 | (6-ounce) can tomato paste |
| | Oregano to taste |
| | Basil to taste |
| 1 | red bell pepper, chopped (may be roasted) |
| 1 | yellow bell pepper, chopped (may be roasted) |
| 8 | ounces fresh mushrooms, sliced |
| 4 | ounces feta cheese, crumbled |
| 2 | pounds small shrimp, cooked, peeled |
| 1 | cup grated Parmesan cheese |
| 12 | ounces mozzarella cheese, shredded |

# Downtown Vegetables & Sides

## Columns in Black

From 1816 to 1821, eight "little palaces" were erected in downtown Savannah that would change the face of the city. They were the work of a young English architect named William Jay. Today, architectural scholars tell us they are among the finest Regency buildings ever built in the United States. The city's wealthiest and most influential citizens hired Mr. Jay to build their dream homes. Two of those houses, the Owens-Thomas and Telfair mansions, are today open to visitors, who marvel at the faux finishes, curved walls, and trompe l'oeil of Jay's sumptuous interiors. However, it is the Scarbrough House that most exemplifies Savannah hospitality.

Perhaps it's because Julia Scarbrough, known as "the Countess," was one of the great hostesses of the era. President Monroe was a guest at one of her famous balls, and she had red carpet laid in the streets of Savannah between the theater and her house so that the female guests would not ruin their slippers in the city's sandy streets. Somehow it is not surprising that her husband, who was a backer of the world's first steamship to cross any ocean (the S.S. Savannah), eventually went bankrupt.

*The columned portico drawing is the circular colonnade of the Archibald Bulloch House, which stood on the southwest trust lot of Orleans Square. Though razed in 1916, its majestic portico influenced a host of others that still stand, including the Hull-Barrow House on the southwest trust lot of Chippewa Square and the McNeil House on Whitaker Street.*

# Vegetables & Sides

Columns in Black   *by H. Alexander Buffalo*
*Sequential Art Graduate Student, The Savannah College of Art and Design*

# Asparagus with Orange Glaze

Arrange the asparagus in a shallow dish. Combine the orange juice, orange zest, sugar, ginger and soy sauce in a bowl and mix well. Pour over the asparagus, turning to coat. Marinate, covered, in the refrigerator for 2 hours or longer, turning occasionally. Drain, reserving the marinade. Arrange the asparagus on a baking sheet. Broil for 5 minutes or until tender-crisp; do not overcook. Heat the reserved marinade in a saucepan over high heat until reduced by $1/2$, stirring frequently. Pour over the asparagus on a serving platter. Yield: 6 servings.

2   pounds fresh asparagus, trimmed
1/2   cup orange juice
    Zest of 1 orange
1   tablespoon sugar
1   tablespoon minced fresh ginger
1   tablespoon soy sauce

# Trustees Garden Asparagus

Fry the bacon in a skillet until crisp. Drain, reserving the pan drippings. Crumble the bacon. Stir-fry the asparagus and garlic in the reserved pan drippings in the skillet for 5 to 7 minutes. Add the water chestnuts. Stir-fry for 1 to 2 minutes longer or until of the desired degree of crispness. Season with the garlic salt. Spoon into a serving bowl; top with the bacon. Serve immediately. Yield: 4 servings.

4   to 6 slices bacon
1   pound asparagus, cut up
1   clove of garlic, finely minced
1/2   cup water chestnuts, drained, sliced
1/2   teaspoon garlic salt (optional)

# Broughton Baked Beans

8 ounces bacon
3 or 4 Vidalia onions or large mild onions, chopped
1¹/₄ cups packed brown sugar
1 teaspoon Dijon mustard
¹/₂ cup apple cider vinegar
2 (16-ounce) cans baked beans
2 (16-ounce) cans butter beans, drained
1 (16-ounce) can red kidney beans, drained

*Nice change from traditional baked beans.*

Fry the bacon in a skillet until crisp. Drain, reserving 2 tablespoons of the pan drippings. Crumble the bacon. Sauté the onions in the reserved pan drippings in a saucepan until tender. Stir in the brown sugar, Dijon mustard and cider vinegar. Add the baked beans, butter beans and kidney beans and mix well. Fold in the bacon. Spoon into a 2¹/₂- to 3-quart baking dish sprayed with nonstick cooking spray. Bake at 300 degrees for 1 hour or until bubbly. Yield: 6 servings.

# Green Beans in Warm Marinade

¹/₂ cup slivered almonds
1 pound green beans, trimmed
1 large shallot, chopped
¹/₄ cup raspberry or balsamic vinegar
¹/₄ cup olive oil
2 tablespoons chopped fresh parsley
Salt and pepper to taste

Arrange the almonds on a baking sheet. Toast in a moderate oven for 10 minutes, stirring occasionally. Combine the green beans with enough water to cover in a saucepan. Bring to a boil. Boil for 3 to 6 minutes or until of the desired degree of crispness; drain. Combine the shallot, raspberry vinegar, olive oil and parsley in a bowl and mix well. Add the green beans, stirring to coat. Stir in the almonds, salt and pepper. Serve immediately. Yield: 4 servings.

# Lemon Green Beans

Cut 4 thin slices from the lemon. Squeeze the juice from the remaining lemon into a bowl. Bring the water and salt to a boil in a saucepan. Add the green beans; reduce heat. Simmer, covered, for 20 to 30 minutes or until tender; drain. Sauté the onion in the butter in a skillet for 2 to 3 minutes. Add the green beans, lemon juice and brown sugar. Cook just until heated through, stirring constantly. Spoon into a 2-quart serving bowl or onto a serving platter. Top with the lemon slices. Yield: 4 servings.

1   large lemon
3   cups water
1/2 teaspoon salt
1   pound fresh green beans, cut into 1 1/2-inch pieces
1   small onion, sliced, separated into rings
3   tablespoons melted butter or margarine
1   teaspoon brown sugar

# Steamed Sesame Ginger Broccoli

*Hot and spicy!*

Separate the broccoli into florets, discarding the stems. Steam in a vegetable steamer for 5 minutes. Press the ginger through a garlic press to extract the juice, discarding the pulp. Combine the ginger juice, garlic, lime juice, soy sauce, sesame oil, hot chili oil and sugar in a bowl and mix well. Pour over the broccoli in a serving bowl; drizzle with the butter. Top with the sesame seeds. Serve immediately. Yield: 3 to 4 servings.

1 1/2 pounds broccoli
3   tablespoons finely grated ginger
1   medium clove of garlic, crushed
2   tablespoons fresh lime juice
2   teaspoons soy sauce
2   teaspoons sesame oil
1/2 teaspoon hot chili oil
1/2 teaspoon sugar
1   tablespoon melted butter
2   teaspoons sesame seeds

# Carrots in Vermouth

2   tablespoons butter or olive oil
2   pounds carrots, julienned
1/4   cup sweet vermouth
    Salt and freshly ground pepper
    to taste
2   tablespoons chopped fresh
    parsley

*Nice, elegant and great for dinner parties.*

Heat the butter or olive oil in a skillet until hot. Add the carrots. Sauté just until the carrots begin to brown. Stir in the vermouth. Simmer for 5 minutes, stirring often. Season with salt and pepper. Spoon into a serving bowl. Sprinkle with the parsley. Yield: 6 to 8 servings.

# Roasted Eggplant with Peppers and Cucumber

1 1/2   pounds eggplant
1/2   cup chopped red bell pepper
1/2   cup chopped yellow bell pepper
1/2   cup chopped cucumber
1   tablespoon chopped fresh parsley
2   tablespoons extra-virgin
    olive oil
2   tablespoons fresh lemon juice
1/2   teaspoon minced garlic
    Salt and freshly ground pepper
    to taste

Roast the whole eggplant on a grill; a gas burner or a broiler may be used. Roast until the skin is blistered and charred on all sides and the eggplant is soft to the touch, turning frequently. Let stand until cool. Peel and cut into 1-inch or smaller strips; discard seeds as desired. Place in a colander. Drain for 30 minutes or until no more liquid is being released. Combine the eggplant, red pepper, yellow pepper, cucumber and parsley in a bowl and mix gently. Add the olive oil, lemon juice and garlic, tossing gently to coat. Season with salt and pepper just before serving. Yield: 6 to 8 servings.

# Grilled Leeks with Orange Chive Butter

For the Orange Chive Butter, combine the butter, chives, zest, orange juice, salt and pepper in a bowl and mix well. Trim the leeks 2 inches beyond the point where the leaves begin to darken. Trim the root end, keeping the base intact. Slit the leeks from top to bottom, leaving the base intact. Soak the leeks in cold water to loosen dirt. Rinse in cold water and drain. Arrange the leeks in a single layer in a steamer basket. Place the basket over boiling water. Steam, covered, for 10 to 12 minutes or until the tip of a knife inserted in the thickest portion of the leek meets no resistance. Grill over hot coals for 2 minutes or until light brown; turn. Grill until light brown. Arrange the leeks on a serving platter. Spread with the Orange Chive Butter.
Yield: 4 servings.

| | |
|---|---|
| 2 | tablespoons unsalted butter, softened |
| 2 | teaspoons snipped fresh chives |
| 1¹/₂ | teaspoons orange zest |
| 1 | teaspoon fresh orange juice |
| ¹/₄ | teaspoon salt |
| ¹/₄ | teaspoon freshly ground pepper |
| 4 | leeks, small to medium thickness |

# Mushroom Florentine

*A nice side dish served with pork tenderloin.*

Cook the spinach using package directions adding 1 teaspoon salt; drain. Sprinkle with garlic powder. Sauté the onion in the butter in a skillet until tender. Remove the onion with a slotted spoon and add to the spinach, reserving the pan drippings; mix well. Spread the spinach mixture in a greased 9x12-inch baking dish. Sprinkle with the cheese. Sauté the mushrooms in the reserved pan drippings. Season with garlic powder. Spread over the spinach layer. Bake at 350 degrees for 20 to 25 minutes. Yield: 6 to 8 servings.

| | |
|---|---|
| 4 | (10-ounce) packages frozen chopped spinach |
| 1 | teaspoon salt |
| | Garlic powder to taste |
| ¹/₂ | cup chopped onion |
| ¹/₂ | cup butter |
| 1 | cup shredded sharp Cheddar cheese |
| 2 | pounds fresh mushrooms, sliced |

# Mushroom Pie

2  large onions, coarsely chopped
1/2  cup butter or margarine
3  pounds mushrooms, sliced
2  tablespoons butter or
   margarine
2  tablespoons flour
1  cup strong chicken stock
1/2  cup madeira or dry sherry
3/4  teaspoon celery salt
1/2  teaspoon ground black pepper
1/8  teaspoon cayenne
1  readymade pie pastry or 1
   recipe (1-crust) pie pastry

Sauté the onions in 1/2 cup butter in a skillet until golden brown. Remove with a slotted spoon to a bowl, reserving the pan drippings. Sauté the mushrooms in the reserved pan drippings for 10 minutes or until tender. Arrange the onions and mushrooms in a 10-inch pie plate or shallow baking dish. Heat 2 tablespoons butter in a saucepan until melted. Stir in the flour until blended. Cook over low heat for 2 minutes, stirring constantly. Add the chicken stock gradually and mix well. Cook until thickened, stirring constantly. Stir in the wine, celery salt, black pepper and cayenne. Pour over the onion mixture. Roll the pie pastry on a lightly floured surface to fit the pie plate or baking dish. Arrange over the prepared layers; crimp the edge. Place a pie bird in the center of the pastry or cut vents with a sharp knife. Bake at 375 degrees for 30 minutes or until brown and bubbly. May prepare in advance, store in the refrigerator, and bake just before serving. Let stand at room temperature for 1 hour before baking. Yield: 12 servings.

# Grilled Okra

2  dozen whole okra pods
1  cup olive oil
1/2  cup soy sauce
2  tablespoons lemon pepper
2  cloves of garlic, crushed

*A new way to serve okra.*

Rinse the okra and pat dry. Arrange in a shallow dish. Combine the olive oil, soy sauce, lemon pepper and garlic in a bowl and mix well. Pour over the okra, turning to coat. Marinate at room temperature for 1 hour, turning occasionally. Drain, discarding the marinade. Grill over medium-hot coals for 15 minutes or until done to taste, turning frequently. Yield: 4 to 6 servings.

# Vidalia Onion Pie

Fry the bacon in a skillet until crisp. Drain the bacon on paper towels, reserving the pan drippings. Crumble the bacon. Sauté the onion in the reserved pan drippings in the skillet. Stir in the bacon. Sprinkle with the flour and mix well. Remove from heat. Combine the eggs and milk in a bowl, beating until blended. Add the bacon mixture and mix well. Season with the salt and pepper. Sprinkle the Swiss cheese and Parmesan cheese over the bottom of the pie shell. Pour the milk mixture into the prepared pie shell. Bake at 350 degrees for 1 hour. Yield: 4 to 5 servings.

8   to 12 slices bacon
1   large Vidalia onion, chopped
2$^1$/2 to 3 tablespoons flour
2   eggs, beaten
1   cup milk
$^1$/2 teaspoon salt, or to taste
$^1$/2 teaspoon pepper, or to taste
$^1$/4 to $^1$/2 cup shredded Swiss cheese
$^1$/4 to $^1$/2 cup grated Parmesan cheese
1   unbaked (9-inch) pie shell

# Vidalia Onion Torte

*Sometimes summer onions can be juicy—consider this when making this dish as it affects the consistency. If it turns out to be soupy, use as a dip and serve with chips or assorted crackers.*

Pat the onions with paper towels to remove excess moisture. Combine the onions, cream cheese, Parmesan cheese and mayonnaise in a bowl and mix well. Spoon into a pie plate or quiche pan. Bake at 425 degrees for 15 minutes or until golden brown. Yield: 15 to 20 servings.

4   cups chopped Vidalia onions
24   ounces cream cheese, softened
2   cups freshly grated Parmesan cheese
$^1$/2 cup mayonnaise

# New Potatoes with Basil

10  small to medium new red
    potatoes, cut into quarters
1/4  cup butter
2   tablespoons vegetable oil
1/2  onion, chopped
1/4  cup chopped fresh basil, or
    1 tablespoon dried basil
3   tablespoons chopped fresh
    parsley, or 1 tablespoon dried
    parsley
1 1/2  teaspoons salt
1   teaspoon oregano
1/4  cup chopped roasted red bell
    pepper (optional)
    Pepper to taste

Place potatoes in a pan of boiling water. Cook for 15 minutes or just until tender; drain. Heat the butter and oil in a saucepan until hot. Add the potatoes, onion, basil, parsley, salt, oregano, red pepper and pepper, tossing to mix.
Yield: 4 servings.

# New Potatoes in Red Pepper Oil

1 1/2  pounds small new potatoes,
    scrubbed
1   clove of garlic, chopped
1/3  cup olive oil
1/2  teaspoon crushed dried red
    pepper
1   medium red bell pepper, thinly
    sliced
1/2  to 1 teaspoon salt
1   tablespoon chopped scallion

Place potatoes in a pan of boiling water. Cook for 20 minutes or until tender; drain. Sauté the garlic in the olive oil in a skillet over medium heat for 2 minutes. Add the red pepper and red bell pepper and mix well. Sauté for 3 to 5 minutes or until the bell pepper is tender. Add the potatoes, stirring gently to coat. Sprinkle with the salt. Spoon into a serving bowl. Sprinkle with the scallion.
Yield: 6 to 8 servings.

# Potatoes Gruyère

Layer half the potatoes in a buttered 9x12-inch baking dish. Sprinkle with half the salt, pepper, cheese and butter. Repeat. Pour the stock over the prepared layers. Bake at 425 degrees for 40 to 50 minutes or until the potatoes are tender and golden brown. Serve immediately.
Yield: 6 servings.

8   medium potatoes, peeled, thinly sliced
3/4   teaspoon salt
1/4   teaspoon pepper
1 1/4   cups grated Gruyère cheese or shredded Swiss cheese
6   tablespoons butter, chopped
1   cup chicken stock

# Potato Salad St. Julian

*Mingling of flavors makes a divine dish.*

Combine the mayonnaise, Dijonnaise, vinegar, dill or parsley, salt and pepper in a bowl and mix well. Fold in the red potatoes, celery and green onions. Chill, covered, overnight.  Yield: 4 to 6 servings.

1   cup mayonnaise
1/4   cup Dijonnaise
2   tablespoons vinegar
2   tablespoons chopped fresh dill or parsley
1/2   teaspoon salt
1/4   teaspoon pepper
2   pounds red potatoes, cooked, peeled, cubed
1   cup chopped celery
1/2   cup chopped green onions

# Red Peppers with Corn

2   or 3 ears of corn or 1 cup frozen
    corn
2   red bell peppers
1   tablespoon olive oil
1   tablespoon butter
1/3   cup finely chopped scallions
1   to 2 cloves of garlic, minced
1/8   teaspoon cumin
    Salt and pepper to taste

Scrape the corn kernels into a bowl. Cut the red peppers into thin slices 1 to 2 inches in length. Heat the olive oil and butter in a skillet until hot. Add the corn, red peppers and scallions and mix well. Sprinkle with the garlic, cumin, salt and pepper. Cook for 1 to 2 minutes, stirring constantly. Spoon into a heated serving bowl. Serve immediately. Yield: 4 servings.

# Fresh Spinach with Apple, Onion and Pear

1/4   cup white wine vinegar
1/4   cup dry sherry or apple juice
2   tablespoons honey
1   tablespoon lemon juice
1/8   teaspoon salt
1/8   teaspoon pepper
1/8   teaspoon thyme
1   onion, sliced, separated into
    rings
1   tablespoon olive oil
1   pear, sliced
1   apple, sliced
1   (10-ounce) package fresh
    spinach, trimmed

Combine the wine vinegar, sherry, honey, lemon juice, salt, pepper and thyme in a bowl and mix well. Sauté the onion in the olive oil in a skillet over medium-high heat until tender. Add the pear and apple slices and the honey mixture and mix well. Cook for 5 to 6 minutes or until the fruit is tender-crisp and the sauce is slightly thickened, stirring frequently. Arrange the spinach on a serving platter; top with the fruit mixture. Yield: 4 servings.

# Baked Zucchini, Tomatoes, Red Onion and Basil

*Nice served with grilled fish or chicken and rice.*

Soak the red onion in enough ice water to cover in a bowl for 30 minutes; drain. Sauté the zucchini in 2 tablespoons olive oil in a skillet just until the squash begins to change color. Season with salt and pepper. Transfer to a bowl using a slotted spoon, reserving the pan drippings. Add 1 tablespoon olive oil to the pan drippings. Heat until hot. Add the onion and balsamic vinegar. Sauté until tender. Season with salt and pepper. Layer the zucchini, onion, tomatoes and basil in a buttered au gratin dish. Drizzle with the remaining 3 tablespoons olive oil. Bake at 375 degrees for 30 to 45 minutes or until brown and bubbly, basting several times with the juices from the vegetables. Yield: 8 servings.

1   medium red onion, sliceed
3   or 4 large zucchini, cut
    lengthwise into slices
6   tablespoons extra-virgin
    olive oil, divided
    *Salt and pepper to taste*
1   tablespoon balsamic vinegar
4   large tomatoes, cut into
    quarters
1   large bunch basil, chopped

# Squash and Shrimp

3   pounds yellow squash, sliced
1   pound shrimp, peeled
¼   cup butter
1   bunch spring onions, chopped
    Salt and pepper to taste
½   cup buttered cracker crumbs

Combine the squash with enough water to cover in a saucepan. Cook until tender; drain. Combine the squash, shrimp, butter, spring onions, salt and pepper in a saucepan and mix well. Cook for 15 minutes or until the shrimp turn pink, stirring frequently. Spoon into a 2-quart baking dish; sprinkle with the cracker crumbs. Bake at 350 degrees for 30 minutes. Yield: 8 servings.

# Scalloped Fresh Tomatoes

½   cup finely chopped onion
1   clove of garlic, minced
3   to 4 tablespoons butter
1   cup soft bread crumbs
1   cup grated Parmesan cheese
2   teaspoons chopped fresh basil
1   teaspoon sugar
¼   teaspoon salt
⅛   teaspoon pepper
3   or 4 tomatoes, sliced

Sauté the onion and garlic in the butter in a skillet. Stir in the bread crumbs, cheese, basil, sugar, salt and pepper. Cook for 2 to 3 minutes, stirring constantly. Layer the tomatoes and bread crumb mixture ⅓ at a time in a greased 1-quart shallow baking dish. Bake at 350 degrees for 20 to 30 minutes or until brown and bubbly. May add sliced Vidalia onions between each layer. Yield: 4 servings.

# Fried Green Tomatoes with Tomato Conserve

Cut the tomatoes into ¹/₄- to ¹/₂-inch slices.
Sprinkle with salt and pepper. Spread the flour on
a plate; season with salt and pepper. Coat each
side of the tomato slices with the seasoned flour.
Heat the butter in a heavy skillet until melted. Add
the tomatoes. Cook until golden brown on both
sides, turning once; drain on paper towels. Serve
with Tomato Conserve. Yield: 20 to 24 servings.

3   or 4 green tomatoes
    *Salt and freshly ground pepper*
    *to taste*
1   *cup flour or cornmeal*
¹/₂ *to 1 cup butter*
³/₄ *cup Tomato Conserve*

## Tomato Conserve

Combine the tomatoes, cider vinegar, 1 cup sugar,
salt and pepper in a heavy saucepan and mix well.
Simmer for 1¹/₂ hours or until thickened and the
mixture clings to a spoon, stirring occasionally.
Stir in ¹/₂ cup sugar if desired. May freeze for
future use. Yield: 1 quart.

8   *pounds fresh tomatoes, peeled,*
    *cut into quarters*
2   *cups apple cider vinegar*
1   *to 1¹/₂ cups sugar*
    *Salt and pepper to taste*

# Tomato Pie in Biscuit Crust

<sup>1</sup>/4  cup butter
2<sup>1</sup>/2  cups self-rising flour
<sup>2</sup>/3  cup milk
5  or 6 ripe tomatoes
2  tablespoons torn fresh basil
1  tablespoon torn fresh chives
   Salt and pepper to taste
1<sup>1</sup>/2  cups shredded sharp Cheddar
   cheese
<sup>1</sup>/3  cup mayonnaise

*Biscuit crust is a must!*

Cut the butter into the flour in a bowl until crumbly. Add the milk, stirring until of the consistency of a medium dough. Knead on a lightly floured surface. Divide the dough into 2 equal portions. Roll each portion on a lightly floured surface to fit a 9-inch pie plate. Line the pie plate with half the pastry. Place the tomatoes in boiling water and boil for 10 seconds. Remove with a slotted spoon. Let stand until cool. Peel and slice. Arrange the tomatoes in the prepared pie plate. Sprinkle with the basil, chives, salt, pepper and <sup>1</sup>/2 of the cheese. Spread with the mayonnaise; sprinkle with the remaining cheese. Top with the remaining pastry, sealing and fluting the edge and cutting vents. Bake at 400 degrees for 20 minutes or until brown. May use your favorite biscuit recipe for the crust. Do not use a commercial pie shell, as the pastry is too thin and flaky.
Yield: 6 servings.

# Tomato Tart

*Delicious way to serve tomatoes.*

Sprinkle the tomatoes with salt to taste. Place in a colander. Drain for 30 minutes. Remove seeds. Pat dry with paper towels. Combine the flour and ¹/₂ teaspoon salt in a bowl and mix well. Cut in the butter until crumbly. Add the cold water 1 tablespoon at a time, mixing well with a fork after each addition. Turn onto a lightly floured surface. Roll to fit a 10-inch pie plate or tart pan. Fit into the pie plate or tart pan; trim the edge. Place in the freezer and freeze for 30 minutes. Spread the Dijon mustard over the prepared pastry. Sprinkle with the basil; top with the cheese. Arrange the tomato slices over the cheese. Beat the whipping cream, eggs and pepper in a mixer bowl until blended. Pour over the prepared layers. Bake at 350 degrees for 30 minutes. Cool for 10 minutes. Cut into slices. Yield: 8 to 10 servings.

3　large tomatoes, cut into ¹/₂-inch slices, seeded
　　Salt to taste
1¹/₂ cups flour
¹/₂　teaspoon salt
¹/₄　cup unsalted butter or shortening, chilled, cut into small pieces
3　to 4 tablespoons cold water
2　tablespoons Dijon mustard
3　tablespoons chopped fresh basil
4　ounces mozzarella cheese, cut into 8 thin slices
1　cup whipping cream
2　eggs
　　Freshly ground pepper to taste

# Marinated Grilled Vegetables

<sup></sup>

| | |
|---|---|
| ¹/₂ | cup balsamic vinegar |
| ¹/₄ | cup olive oil |
| 2 | tablespoons white wine |
| 1 | tablespoon chopped shallot |
| 1 | teaspoon minced garlic |
| 1 | teaspoon pepper |
| 1 | teaspoon salt |
| 1 | pound fresh asparagus |
| 4 | unpeeled new potatoes, parboiled |
| 4 | Roma tomatoes |
| 3 | zucchini, sliced lengthwise |
| 2 | purple or Vidalia onions, cut into quarters |
| 4 | whole portobello mushrooms |
| 1 | red bell pepper, cut into quarters |
| 1 | yellow bell pepper, cut into quarters |
| 1 | tablespoon chopped fresh chives |
| 1 | tablespoon chopped fresh rosemary |
| 1 | tablespoon chopped fresh parsley |

Combine the balsamic vinegar, olive oil, white wine, shallot, garlic, pepper and salt in a bowl and mix well. Arrange the asparagus, new potatoes, tomatoes, zucchini, onions, mushrooms, red pepper and yellow pepper in a shallow dish. Pour the vinegar mixture over the vegetables, turning to coat. Marinate at room temperature for several hours, turning occasionally. Drain, reserving the marinade. Grill the vegetables over hot coals for 12 to 14 minutes or until of the desired degree of crispness, turning once. Transfer the vegetables to a serving platter; drizzle with the reserved marinade. Sprinkle with the chives, rosemary and parsley. May substitute your favorite vegetables for the ones mentioned. This marinade is excellent to use for portobello mushrooms before grilling. Yield: 8 servings.

# Linguini con Verdure

*This recipe was contributed by Il Pasticcio.*

Soak the mushrooms in sherry in a bowl. Drain and chop. Cook the broccoli, cauliflower, asparagus and black olives in boiling salted water in a saucepan for 3 to 5 minutes. Drain and rinse with cold water. Cook the peas in boiling salted water for $1^1/2$ minutes. Drain and rinse under cold water. Cut the broccoli, cauliflower and asparagus into $1^1/2$-inch pieces. Cook the mushrooms, nutmeg and basil in $1/2$ cup plus $1^1/2$ teaspoons butter in a saucepan for 5 minutes, stirring frequently. Add the broccoli, cauliflower, asparagus, black olives and peas and mix well. Cook for 5 minutes longer, stirring occasionally. Stir in the whipping cream, pinch of salt and white pepper. Simmer for 3 minutes, stirring occasionally. Combine the linguini and $3^1/2$ tablespoons butter in a bowl and mix until coated. Add the broccoli mixture, tossing to mix. Add $1/2$ of the cheese and mix gently. Spoon onto a serving platter. Sprinkle with white pepper and the remaining cheese. Top with the marinara sauce. Yield: 4 servings.

10  pieces dried porcini or shiitake mushrooms
Dry sherry
Florets of 1 small bunch broccoli
10  cauliflowerets
14  asparagus tips
$1/2$  cup sliced black olives
Salt to taste
1  cup fresh or frozen peas
Pinch of nutmeg
4  fresh basil leaves, chopped
$1/2$  cup plus $1^1/2$ teaspoons butter
$3/4$  cup whipping cream
Pinch of salt
Ground white pepper to taste
$1^1/2$  pounds fresh linguini, cooked al dente, drained
$3^1/2$  tablespoons melted butter
$3/4$  cup freshly grated Parmesan cheese
$3/4$  cup marinara sauce, heated (optional)

# Red Pepper Pasta Stir-Fry

Stir-fry the vegetables in the oil in a skillet for 7 to 8 minutes. Add the pasta and stir-fry sauce and mix well. Stir-fry just until heated through. Spoon onto a serving platter. Sprinkle with the cashews. Serve immediately. Yield: 4 servings.

1  (16-ounce) package frozen stir-fry vegetables
1  tablespoon vegetable oil
9  ounces hot red pepper tortellini, cooked, drained
$3/4$  cup peanut stir-fry sauce
$1/4$  cup unsalted cashews

# Baked Deviled Eggs

8   eggs, hard-cooked
1   (3-ounce) can mushroom
    pieces, drained
    Mayonnaise to taste
1¹/2 teaspoons prepared mustard
6   tablespoons butter
6   tablespoons flour
2   cups cream
2   cups milk
¹/2  teaspoon salt
1   (10-ounce) package frozen
    spinach, cooked, drained
    Grated Parmesan cheese
    to taste

*Traditional Easter lunch dish.*

Slice the eggs lengthwise into halves. Remove the yolks carefully, reserving the whites. Combine the yolks, mushrooms, mayonnaise and prepared mustard in a bowl and mix well. Spoon into the reserved egg whites. Arrange in a 9x13-inch baking dish. Heat the butter in a saucepan until melted. Stir in the flour until blended. Add the cream and milk gradually and mix well. Cook until thickened, stirring constantly. Season with the salt. Squeeze the moisture from the spinach. Stir the spinach into the cream sauce. Spoon over the eggs. Sprinkle with Parmesan cheese. Bake at 350 degrees for 25 minutes.
Yield: 8 to 10 servings.

# Spicy Grits

2   cups cold water
¹/2  cup grits
¹/2  teaspoon salt (optional)
¹/2  cup chopped green bell pepper or
    green chiles
¹/2  cup chopped onion
¹/2  cup butter
1   cup shredded sharp Cheddar
    cheese
1   cup milk
2   eggs, beaten
1   teaspoon chili powder
    Shredded Cheddar cheese
    to taste

Combine the cold water, grits and salt in a saucepan and mix well. Bring to a boil, stirring occasionally; reduce heat. Simmer for 6 minutes. Remove from heat. Sauté the green pepper and onion in the butter in a skillet until tender. Stir into the grits. Add 1 cup cheese, milk, eggs and chili powder and mix well. Spoon into a 1-quart baking dish. Bake at 350 degrees for 45 minutes or until the center is firm, sprinkling with cheese to taste 5 minutes before the end of the cooking process.
Yield: 4 to 6 servings.

# New City Market Rice

*Nice accompaniment for beef . . . zippy, zesty taste.*

Sauté the rice, onion and garlic in the oil in a skillet until light brown; drain. Bring the broth, parsley, jalapeño and salt to a boil in a saucepan. Add to the rice mixture and mix well. Simmer, tightly covered, for 25 minutes; do not remove lid while cooking. Yield: 2 to 4 servings.

| | |
|---|---|
| 1 | cup rice |
| 1 | small onion, chopped |
| 1 | clove of garlic, minced |
| 1/4 | cup vegetable oil |
| 2 1/2 | cups chicken broth |
| 1 | tablespoon chopped fresh parsley |
| 1 | jalapeño, minced |
| 1 | teaspoon salt |

# Old City Market Rice

Bring the water to a boil in a saucepan. Add the rice, 2 tablespoons butter and salt and mix well; reduce heat. Simmer, covered, for 20 minutes. Sauté the onion in 2 tablespoons butter in a skillet. Stir into the rice. Layer the rice mixture, green chiles, Monterey Jack cheese and sour cream 1/2 at a time in a greased 1 1/2-quart baking dish. Sprinkle with the Cheddar cheese. Bake at 350 degrees for 20 to 30 minutes or until bubbly. Yield: 6 to 8 servings.

| | |
|---|---|
| 2 1/2 | cups water |
| 1 | cup rice |
| 4 | tablespoons butter, divided |
| 1/2 | teaspoon salt |
| 1 | small onion, chopped |
| 3 | (4-ounce) cans mild whole green chiles, drained, chopped |
| 1 | pound Monterey Jack cheese, sliced |
| 1 | cup sour cream |
| 2 | cups shredded sharp Cheddar cheese |

# Downtown Breads

## Hall Street Estate

In Savannah, the Victorian District is a geographical area lying south of
Gaston Street and has a distinctly different look than the Historic District.
Gingerbread and wedding-cake houses abound, along with the darker
and more imposing Romanesque style.

The center of this area of architectural fancy is the twenty-acre spread of
Forsyth Park, an azalea-bedecked oasis anchored by a beautiful white fountain
erected in 1858. The park today is a gathering place for those enjoying frisbee
throwing, jogging, rollerblading, and sun worshipping, or the more cultural
festivals of Shakespeare, jazz, and art. It's also the site of one of the city's
most popular events, the Savannah Symphony's Picnic in the Park.

The Picnic, held on a crisp fall evening, is a tribute to both beautiful music
and fine food. During the orchestra's performance of light classics, a favorite
audience activity is observing various picnic arrangements. While bare bones
picnics are sometimes spotted, it is not unusual in the least to see linen-bedecked
tables topped with sterling, crystal, and fresh flowers. Silver candelabra and
ice-filled wine buckets are the norm; and some people have been known to
tent their party, wear black tie, and hire caterers—with waiters.

Most participants, though, are content to gather their friends on a blanket
and share hampers of magnificent food prepared in their own kitchens. It's just
one more way to enjoy entertaining, Downtown Savannah Style.

The drawing at right details a doorway of a beautiful Victorian double house
built in 1872 on Hall Street, which intersects Forsyth Park near the fountain.

# Breads

Hall Street Estate  *by Catherine Myler Fruisen*
*Illustration Graduate Student, The Savannah College of Art and Design*

# Blueberry Bread

Sift the flour, baking powder and salt together. Beat the butter, sugar and eggs in a bowl until light and fluffy. Add the dry ingredients alternately with the milk, beating at low speed after each addition until blended. Fold in the blueberries. Spoon into a greased 8x8-inch pan. Sprinkle with the brown sugar and cinnamon. Bake at 375 degrees for 35 minutes. Serve warm. Yield: 12 servings.

2   cups sifted flour
1   tablespoon baking powder
1/2   teaspoon salt
1/2   cup butter, softened
1/2   cup sugar
2   eggs
3/4   cup milk
1   cup blueberries
2   tablespoons light brown sugar
1/2   teaspoon cinnamon

# Poppy Seed Bread

*The flavor of this bread is best when served warm.*

Combine the flour, baking powder, sugar and salt in a bowl and mix well. Cut in the butter until crumbly. Stir in the cheese and poppy seeds. Add the milk, eggs and prepared mustard, stirring just until moistened. Spoon into a greased and floured 5x9-inch loaf pan. Bake at 350 degrees for 1 1/4 hours or until golden brown. Cool for 5 minutes. Slice and serve warm. Yield: 1 loaf.

3 1/2 cups flour
5   teaspoons baking powder
1   tablespoon sugar
1/2   teaspoon salt
1/3   cup butter
2   cups shredded Swiss cheese
1   tablespoon poppy seeds
1 1/2 cups milk
2   eggs, lightly beaten
2   teaspoons prepared mustard

# Lemon Tea Loaf

3/4 cup milk
1 tablespoon chopped fresh lemon balm or 1 tablespoon lemon juice
1 tablespoon chopped fresh lemon thyme, or 1/4 teaspoon dried thyme
2 cups flour
1 1/2 teaspoons baking powder
1/4 teaspoon salt
1/2 cup butter or margarine, softened
1 cup sugar
2 eggs
1 tablespoon grated lemon peel

**Glaze**
1 cup sifted confectioners' sugar
2 tablespoons lemon juice

Bring the milk, lemon balm and lemon thyme to a boil in a saucepan. Remove from heat. Let stand, covered, for 5 minutes. Combine the flour, baking powder and salt in a bowl and mix well. Beat the butter in a bowl until creamy, scraping the bowl occasionally. Add the sugar gradually, beating constantly until blended. Add the eggs 1 at a time, beating well after each addition. Add the dry ingredients alternately with the milk mixture, beginning and ending with the dry ingredients and mixing well after each addition. Stir in the lemon peel. Spoon into a greased and floured 5x9-inch loaf pan. Bake at 325 degrees for 50 minutes or until the loaf tests done. Cool in pan on a wire rack for 10 minutes. Invert onto the wire rack to cool completely. Drizzle with a mixture of the confectioners' sugar and lemon juice. Yield: 1 loaf.

# Strawberry and Almond Bread

Beat the sugar and butter in a bowl until creamy, scraping the bowl occasionally. Add the eggs 1 at a time, beating well after each addition. Stir in the almonds, baking powder, almond flavoring, cinnamon, baking soda and salt; batter will be thick. Fold in the strawberries. Add the flour and sour cream alternately, beginning and ending with the flour and mixing well after each addition. Spoon into 2 greased and floured 5x9-inch loaf pans. Bake at 325 degrees for 1 hour and 10 minutes. Cool in pans on a wire rack. Yield: 2 loaves.

| | |
|---|---|
| 2 | cups sugar |
| 1 | cup butter, softened |
| 3 | eggs |
| $^3/_4$ | cup sliced almonds, toasted |
| 2 | teaspoons baking powder |
| $1^1/_2$ | teaspoons almond extract |
| $1^1/_2$ | teaspoons cinnamon |
| 1 | teaspoon baking soda |
| $^1/_4$ | teaspoon salt |
| 2 | cups sliced strawberries |
| 4 | cups flour |
| $^1/_3$ | cup sour cream |

# Sun-Dried Tomato Bread

*Zesty flavor! Good with a light soup or salad.*

Drain and chop the sun-dried tomatoes, reserving 2 tablespoons of the oil. Combine the self-rising flour, cheese, scallions, sun-dried tomatoes, parsley, rosemary and pepper in a bowl and mix well. Whisk the buttermilk, reserved sun-dried tomato oil, vegetable oil, sugar, garlic and eggs in a bowl until mixed. Add to the flour mixture, stirring just until moistened. Spoon into a greased 5x9-inch loaf pan. Bake at 350 degrees for 1 hour or until the loaf tests done. Cool in pan for 5 minutes or longer. Invert onto a wire rack to cool to desired temperature. Serve warm or at room temperature. Yield: 1 loaf.

| | |
|---|---|
| $^1/_3$ | cup sun-dried tomatoes packed in oil |
| $2^1/_2$ | cups self-rising flour |
| 1 | cup shredded Muenster or provolone cheese |
| $^1/_2$ | cup chopped scallions |
| 2 | tablespoons minced fresh parsley |
| 2 | teaspoons rosemary |
| $^1/_2$ | teaspoon coarsely ground pepper |
| $1^1/_4$ | cups buttermilk |
| 2 | tablespoons vegetable oil |
| 2 | tablespoons sugar |
| 2 | cloves of garlic, minced |
| 2 | eggs |

# Whole Wheat Raisin Bread

3¹/₄ cups (about) all-purpose flour
¹/₂ cup sugar
1 tablespoon salt
1¹/₂ teaspoons cinnamon
¹/₂ teaspoon nutmeg
2 envelopes dry yeast
2 cups milk
³/₄ cup water
¹/₄ cup vegetable oil
4 cups whole wheat flour
1¹/₄ cups raisins
1 cup rolled oats
   Melted butter

Combine 2 cups of the all-purpose flour, sugar, salt, cinnamon, nutmeg and yeast in a large bowl and mix well. Heat the milk, water and oil in a saucepan until lukewarm; do not boil. Pour over the flour mixture. Beat at medium speed for 4 minutes, scraping the bowl occasionally. Add the whole wheat flour, raisins and oats, stirring until mixed. Add enough of the remaining all-purpose flour to make a soft dough. Knead on a lightly floured surface until smooth. Place the dough in a greased bowl, turning to coat the surface. Let rise, covered with a tea towel, in a warm place for 1 hour or until doubled in bulk. Punch the dough down; divide into 2 portions. Shape each portion into a loaf in a greased loaf pan. Brush the tops with melted butter. Let rise, covered, for 30 minutes or until doubled in bulk. Bake at 375 degrees for 40 minutes or until the loaves test done. Brush with melted butter. Yield: 2 loaves.

# The Cloister Corn Bread Muffins

*These are a tasty, delightful treat from The Cloister Resort located on Sea Island.*

Fry the bacon in a skillet until crisp; drain. Beat the butter and sugar in a bowl until creamy, scraping the bowl occasionally. Add the eggs 1 at a time, mixing well after each addition. Add the bacon, corn, Cheddar cheese, Monterey Jack cheese, flour, cornmeal, baking powder and salt, stirring just until moistened. Fill greased muffin cups 1/2 full. Bake at 350 degrees for 20 minutes. Yield: 2 dozen muffins.

6   ounces bacon, chopped
3/4  cup butter, softened
1/2  cup sugar
4   eggs
1   (15-ounce) can yellow cream-
    style corn
1   cup shredded Cheddar cheese
1   cup shredded Monterey Jack
    cheese
1   cup flour
1   cup yellow cornmeal
1/4  cup baking powder
1   teaspoon salt

# Georgia Peach Bran Muffins

Combine the self-rising flour, sugar, cinnamon and lemon peel in a bowl and mix well. Combine the cereal and milk in a separate bowl and mix well. Let stand until the milk is absorbed. Stir in the oil and egg. Add to the flour mixture, stirring just until moistened. Fold in the peaches. Fill 36 greased miniature muffin cups or 12 regular muffin cups 2/3 full. Bake at 400 degrees for 20 minutes for the miniature muffins or 25 minutes for the regular muffins.
Yield: 3 dozen miniature muffins or 1 dozen regular muffins.

1   cup self-rising flour
1/3  cup sugar
1/2  teaspoon cinnamon
1/2  teaspoon grated lemon peel
1 1/2  cups whole bran cereal
1   cup milk
1/4  cup vegetable oil
1   egg
1   cup chopped fresh Georgia
    peaches

# Hazelnut-Raspberry Muffins

3   cups sifted flour
4   teaspoons baking powder
1   teaspoon salt
1/4   teaspoon baking soda
2/3   cup packed dark brown sugar
4   ounces hazelnuts, toasted,
      coarsely chopped
2/3   cup orange juice
2/3   cup milk
1/2   cup melted unsalted butter
1   egg, lightly beaten
      Grated zest of 1 orange
1 1/4  cups fresh raspberries

*Nice blend of ingredients. Serve at a luncheon with a main dish salad.*

Sift the flour, baking powder, salt and baking soda into a bowl and mix well. Add the brown sugar and hazelnuts, stirring until the hazelnuts are lightly coated. Add a mixture of the orange juice, milk, butter, egg and orange zest, stirring just until moistened. Fold in the raspberries. Spoon into buttered muffin cups. Bake at 350 degrees for 20 minutes or until golden brown. Decrease the oven temperature to 325 degrees if muffins brown too quickly. May substitute thawed and drained frozen raspberries for the fresh raspberries. Yield: 20 muffins.

# Pecan-Banana Bran Muffins

1   cup flour
1   cup wheat bran
1   teaspoon baking soda
1/2   teaspoon salt
1/2   teaspoon cinnamon
1/2   cup finely chopped pecans
1   cup mashed ripe bananas
1/2   cup unsalted butter, softened
1/2   cup packed brown sugar
1   egg

Combine the flour, wheat bran, baking soda, salt, cinnamon and pecans in a bowl and mix well. Beat the bananas and butter in a mixer bowl until blended. Add the brown sugar and egg, beating until mixed. Add the dry ingredients, stirring just until moistened. Fill muffins cups sprayed with nonstick cooking spray 3/4 full. Bake at 375 degrees for 15 to 20 minutes or until the muffins test done. Cool in pan for 5 minutes.
Yield: 1 dozen muffins.

# Pumpkin-Apple Streusel Muffins

Combine 2¹/₂ cups flour, 2 cups sugar, pumpkin pie spice, baking soda and salt in a bowl and mix well. Combine the pumpkin, oil and eggs in a bowl and mix well. Add to the flour mixture, stirring just until moistened. Fold in the apples. Fill 12 greased or paper-lined muffin cups ³/₄ full. Combine ¹/₄ cup sugar, 2 tablespoons flour and cinnamon in a bowl and mix well. Cut in the butter until crumbly. Sprinkle over the batter. Bake at 350 degrees for 35 to 40 minutes or until the muffins test done. Bake for 40 to 45 minutes for 6 giant muffins. Yield: 1 dozen muffins.

2¹/₂  cups flour
2     cups sugar
1     tablespoon pumpkin pie spice
1     teaspoon baking soda
¹/₄   teaspoon salt
1     cup canned pumpkin
¹/₂   cup vegetable oil
2     eggs, lightly beaten
2     cups finely chopped peeled apples

**Streusel Topping**
¹/₄   cup sugar
2     tablespoons flour
¹/₂   teaspoon cinnamon
4     teaspoons butter

# Parmesan Popovers

Place the oven rack in the next-to-lowest position. Grease 6 muffin cups or custard cups; sprinkle with the Parmesan cheese. Combine the milk, flour, butter and salt in a bowl. Beat in the eggs just until blended; do not overbeat as the volume will be reduced. Fill the prepared muffin cups or custard cups ³/₄ full. Bake at 450 degrees for 15 minutes. Reduce the oven temperature to 350 degrees. Bake for 20 minutes longer. Serve immediately. Do not open the oven door during the cooking process. Yield: 6 popovers.

¹/₄   cup grated Parmesan cheese
1     cup milk
1     cup flour
1     tablespoon melted butter
¹/₄   teaspoon salt
2     eggs

# Sugared Cheese Biscuits

8    ounces sharp Cheddar cheese,
     shredded
1    cup butter, softened
2    cups plus 2 tablespoons flour
3/4  teaspoon paprika
1/2  teaspoon salt
     Confectioners' sugar to taste

*These are wonderful served warm or at room temperature.*

Beat the cheese and butter in a mixer bowl until creamy, scraping the bowl occasionally. Add the flour, paprika and salt and mix well. Shape into 1-inch balls. Place on a baking sheet. Bake at 450 degrees for 7 minutes. Sprinkle confectioners' sugar on a sheet of waxed paper. Place the biscuits on the prepared waxed paper; roll in confectioners' sugar. Serve hot or at room temperature. May be prepared and frozen for future use. Yield: 50 biscuits.

# Bran Rolls

1    envelope dry yeast
1/2  cup lukewarm water
1/2  cup All-Bran
1/3  cup shortening
1/4  cup sugar
1    teaspoon salt
1/2  cup boiling water
1    egg, lightly beaten
3 1/2 cups sifted flour
     Melted butter

*Serve piping hot with lots of butter.*

Dissolve the yeast in the lukewarm water in a large bowl and mix well. Combine the cereal, shortening, sugar and salt in a bowl. Pour the boiling water over the cereal mixture, stirring until the shortening melts. Cool to room temperature. Stir in the egg. Combine with the yeast mixture. Add the flour and mix well. Place in a greased bowl, turning to coat the surface. Chill, covered with waxed paper, in the refrigerator. Let stand at room temperature for 2 to 3 hours before baking. Roll the dough on a lightly floured surface; cut with a biscuit cutter. Brush circles with melted butter. Fold over; pinch edges. Arrange on a baking sheet. Bake at 400 degrees for 15 to 20 minutes or until light brown. Yield: 1 1/2 dozen rolls.

# Sunday Rolls

Dissolve the yeast in the lukewarm water and mix well. Set aside. Combine the oil, sugar and salt in a bowl and mix well. Add the boiling water and mix well. Stir a small amount of the hot mixture into the eggs; stir the eggs into the hot mixture. Add the yeast mixture and mix well. Stir in the flour 1 cup at a time, mixing well after each addition. Let rise, covered with plastic wrap, until doubled in bulk. May be refrigerated overnight. Roll the dough on a lightly floured surface; cut with a cutter. Arrange on a baking sheet; drizzle with melted butter. Let rise, covered with plastic wrap, until doubled in bulk. Bake at 450 degrees for 6 to 10 minutes or until light brown. Yield: 3 dozen rolls.

| | |
|---|---|
| 2 | envelopes dry yeast |
| 1 | cup lukewarm water |
| 1 | cup vegetable oil |
| 1/2 | cup sugar |
| 2 | teaspoons (rounded) salt |
| 1 | cup boiling water |
| 2 | eggs, beaten |
| 6 | cups flour |
| 2 | tablespoons melted butter |

# Puffed Apple Pancake

Combine the eggs, milk, flour, sugar, vanilla, salt and cinnamon in a bowl and mix well; batter will be slightly lumpy. Heat the butter in a 12-inch quiche pan or 9x13-inch baking pan at 425 degrees until melted. Arrange the apple slices over the bottom of the prepared pan. Heat until the butter sizzles; do not burn. Pour the batter over the apples; sprinkle with the brown sugar. Place on the middle oven rack. Bake at 425 degrees for 20 minutes or until puffed and brown. Serve immediately.  Yield: 6 servings.

| | |
|---|---|
| 6 | eggs |
| 1 1/2 | cups milk |
| 1 | cup flour |
| 3 | tablespoons sugar |
| 1 | teaspoon vanilla extract |
| 1/2 | teaspoon salt |
| 1/4 | teaspoon cinnamon |
| 1/2 | cup butter or margarine |
| 2 | apples, peeled, thinly sliced |
| 2 | to 3 tablespoons brown sugar |

# Mocha-Glazed Coffee Cake

**Filling**
| | |
|---|---|
| 6 | tablespoons sugar |
| 3 | tablespoons cinnamon |
| 2 | tablespoons instant coffee granules |
| 2 | tablespoons baking cocoa |

**Cake**
| | |
|---|---|
| 2 | cups flour |
| 1 | teaspoon baking powder |
| $1/2$ | teaspoon salt |
| 2 | cups sugar |
| 1 | cup plus 1 tablespoon butter, softened |
| 2 | eggs |
| $1/2$ | teaspoon vanilla extract |
| 1 | cup plus 2 tablespoons sour cream |

**Glaze**
| | |
|---|---|
| 1 | tablespoon hot water |
| 1 | teaspoon instant coffee granules |
| 4 | ounces cream cheese, softened |
| 6 | tablespoons unsalted butter, softened |
| $1/2$ | cup plus 2 tablespoons sifted confectioners' sugar |
| $1/2$ | teaspoon vanilla extract |
| $1/2$ | teaspoon orange juice |
| | Pinch of salt |

Chopped walnuts

*Delicious and moist! Equally good without the glaze.*

*For the filling,* combine 6 tablespoons sugar, cinnamon, 2 tablespoons coffee granules and baking cocoa in a bowl and mix well. *For the cake,* sift the flour, baking powder and $1/2$ teaspoon salt together. Beat 2 cups sugar and 1 cup plus 1 tablespoon butter in a mixer bowl until creamy. Add the eggs and mix well. Stir in $1/2$ teaspoon vanilla. Add the sifted dry ingredients alternately with the sour cream, beginning and ending with the dry ingredients and mixing well after each addition. Spoon $1/2$ of the batter into a greased and floured bundt pan. Sprinkle with the filling. Top with the remaining batter. Bake at 350 degrees for 50 to 60 minutes or until the coffee cake tests done. Cool in the pan for several minutes. Invert onto a serving plate. *For the glaze,* combine the hot water and 1 teaspoon coffee granules in a bowl, stirring until the coffee granules dissolve. Let stand until cool. Beat the cream cheese and 6 tablespoons butter in a mixer bowl until light and fluffy. Add the confectioners' sugar gradually, beating constantly until blended. Beat in $1/2$ teaspoon vanilla, orange juice, pinch of salt and coffee mixture. Beat for 4 minutes or until doubled in bulk, scraping the bowl occasionally. Spread over the top and side of the coffee cake. Sprinkle with chopped walnuts. Chill, covered, until serving time. Yield: 16 servings.

# Almond Nutmeg Braid

*A beautiful breakfast or brunch bread.*

Dissolve the yeast and 1 teaspoon sugar in the lukewarm water in a large bowl and mix well. Let stand for 5 minutes. Combine the milk, 1/3 cup sugar, 1/4 cup butter, nutmeg and salt in a saucepan. Heat until the butter melts, stirring occasionally. Cool to 110 to 115 degrees. Stir into the yeast mixture. Add the egg and 1 cup of the flour and mix well. Add enough of the remaining flour to make a soft dough and mix well. Knead on a lightly floured surface for 5 minutes or until smooth and elastic. Place the dough in a greased bowl, turning to coat the surface. Let rise, covered loosely, in a warm place for 1 1/2 hours or until doubled in bulk. Punch the dough down. Let rise for 1 hour or until doubled in bulk. Divide into 4 portions. Shape 3 of the portions into 14-inch long ropes. Braid the ropes; pinch the ends to seal. Arrange on a baking sheet. Spread the braid apart in the center. Divide the remaining portion of dough into thirds. Shape each third into a 12-inch long rope; braid and pinch the ends. Place the smaller braid on top of the larger braid. Let rise, covered loosely, for 45 minutes or until doubled in bulk. Bake at 350 degrees for 20 minutes or until the bread tests done. Remove to a wire rack to cool. Combine 1 tablespoon butter, orange juice, lemon juice and orange zest in a saucepan. Heat until the butter melts, stirring occasionally. Stir in enough confectioners' sugar to make of a glaze consistency. Drizzle over the bread; sprinkle with the almonds. Yield: 1 loaf.

1     envelope dry yeast
1     teaspoon sugar
1/4    cup lukewarm
       (110- to 115-degree) water
1/2    cup milk
1/3    cup sugar
1/4    cup unsalted butter
1 1/2 teaspoons nutmeg
1     teaspoon salt
1     egg, beaten
2 3/4 to 3 1/2 cups flour
1     tablespoon unsalted butter
1     tablespoon orange juice
1     tablespoon lemon juice
1     teaspoon grated orange zest
1 1/4 to 1 1/2 cups sifted confectioners'
       sugar
1/4    cup chopped almonds

# Kamish Bread

3 eggs
1 cup sugar
1 cup vegetable oil
3 cups flour
1 teaspoon baking powder
1 cup miniature semisweet
chocolate chips
1/2 cup sugar
1 tablespoon cinnamon

Beat the eggs in a bowl. Stir in 1 cup sugar and oil and mix well. Add a sifted mixture of the flour and baking powder gradually, mixing well. Stir in the chocolate chips. Divide the dough into 3 portions. Shape 2 portions into 1/2-inch-thick rectangles on a baking sheet. Shape the remaining portion into a 1/2-inch-thick rectangle on another baking sheet. Bake at 350 degrees for 15 minutes or until light brown. Cut each rectangle into 1/2-inch slices. Arrange on a baking sheet. Combine 1/2 cup sugar and cinnamon in a bowl and mix well. Sprinkle 1/2 of the sugar mixture over 1 side of the slices. Toast for 5 to 10 minutes; turn. Sprinkle with the remaining sugar mixture. Toast until light brown. Remove to a wire rack to cool. Yield: 3 to 4 dozen.

# Favorite Banana-Chocolate Chip Bread

3 ripe or overripe bananas
1 cup sugar
1/2 cup melted butter or
margarine
2 eggs
1 teaspoon vanilla extract
2 cups flour
1 teaspoon baking soda
1/4 teaspoon salt
1 cup chocolate chips
Chopped nuts to taste
(optional)
Confectioners' sugar

*This can also be made into muffins. Great for dessert or breakfast!*

Process the bananas in a food processor or blender until mashed. Add the sugar, butter, eggs and vanilla. Process until blended. Add the flour, baking soda and salt. Process until blended. Stir in the chocolate chips and nuts. Spoon into a greased 5x9-inch loaf pan. Bake at 350 degrees for 1 hour or until the loaf tests done. Cool in pan for several minutes. Invert onto a wire rack. Sprinkle with confectioners' sugar; wrap in foil. Let stand overnight before serving. May freeze for future use. Yield: 1 loaf.

# Sweet Potato Spoon Bread

*Wonderful way to use leftover holiday sweet potatoes.*

Combine the sweet potatoes, sugar and self-rising flour in a bowl and mix well. Stir in the evaporated milk, butter and eggs. Add the flavorings and nutmeg and mix well. Spoon into a shallow baking pan. Bake at 350 degrees for 30 minutes or until light brown. May substitute two 16-ounce cans of sweet potatoes for the fresh sweet potatoes. Yield: 4 to 6 servings.

| | |
|---|---|
| 2 | cups mashed cooked fresh sweet potatoes |
| 2 | cups sugar |
| 1 | cup self-rising flour |
| 1 | cup evaporated milk |
| 1/2 | cup melted butter |
| 4 | eggs |
| 1 | teaspoon lemon extract |
| 1 | teaspoon vanilla extract |
| 1/2 | teaspoon nutmeg |

# Onion-Cheese French Bread

Beat the butter in a bowl until creamy. Stir in the cheese, mayonnaise and green onions. Spread over the cut sides of the bread. Place on a baking sheet. Broil for 5 minutes or until brown and bubbly. Yield: 10 servings.

| | |
|---|---|
| 1/4 | cup butter, softened |
| 3/4 | cup shredded sharp Cheddar cheese |
| 1/2 | cup mayonnaise |
| 1/4 | cup chopped green onions |
| 1 | loaf French or Italian bread, cut lengthwise into halves |

# Danish Puff

1    *cup butter*
1    *cup sifted flour*
2    *tablespoons water*

**Icing**

1    *cup water*
¹/₂    *cup butter*
1    *cup flour, sifted*
1    *teaspoon almond extract*
3    *eggs*

     *Slivered almonds (optional)*
     *Confectioners' sugar (optional)*
     *Other nuts or fruits (optional)*
     *Cinnamon and sugar*
     *(optional)*

Cut 1 cup butter into 1 cup sifted flour in a bowl until crumbly. Add 2 tablespoons water, stirring until the dough clings together. Press over the bottom of an inverted pizza pan. *For the icing,* bring 1 cup water and ¹/₂ cup butter to a boil in a saucepan. Remove from heat. Add the flour and almond flavoring, stirring constantly until blended. Add the eggs 1 at a time, beating well after each addition. Spread icing over the prepared layer. Bake at 350 degrees for 1 hour and 10 minutes. May sprinkle with slivered almonds, confectioners' sugar, chopped nuts, chopped fruits, or cinnamon and sugar after baking. Yield: 12 servings.

# French Toast Casserole

*Great recipe to prepare in advance for weekend guests.*

Cut the French bread into twenty 1-inch slices. Arrange the slices in 2 rows in a buttered 9x13-inch baking dish, overlapping the slices. Combine the eggs, half-and-half, milk, sugar, vanilla, 1/4 teaspoon cinnamon, 1/4 teaspoon nutmeg and salt in a bowl. Beat with a rotary beater or whisk until blended but not bubbly. Pour evenly over the bread slices, spooning some of the mixture in between the slices. Chill, covered, overnight. *For the topping,* combine the butter, brown sugar, pecans, corn syrup, 1/2 teaspoon cinnamon and 1/2 teaspoon nutmeg in a bowl and mix well. Spread over the bread. Bake at 350 degrees for 40 minutes or until puffed and light brown. Serve with maple syrup or honey. Yield: 6 to 8 servings.

1   (13- to 16-ounce) loaf French bread
8   eggs
2   cups half-and-half
1   cup milk
2   tablespoons sugar
1   teaspoon vanilla extract
1/4   teaspoon cinnamon
1/4   teaspoon nutmeg
    Dash of salt

**Praline Topping**
1   cup butter
1   cup packed light brown sugar
1   cup chopped pecans
2   tablespoons light corn syrup
1/2   teaspoon cinnamon
1/2   teaspoon nutmeg

*Maple syrup or honey*

# Downtown Sweets

## Late Afternoon Sun

*What is it that so captivates visitors and natives alike that our city was called by the French "the most beautiful city in North America"? It's the squares, of course. General Oglethorpe himself artfully laid out the first four even before he arrived in 1733, and the plan was repeated for over one hundred years by city fathers until there were twenty-four squares in all. Three of those were lost to post-World War II "progress," but the remaining squares are zealously guarded and tended. Savannah's system of squares, trust lots, and tything lots has been called the world's most perfect city plan. Here a splashing fountain, there a heroic monument; and everywhere, the lush green landscaping creates a retreat from the modern world. In fact, the enormous quantity of green space creates another phenomenon known as the famous "Savannah Hush"—a quietude that belies location in a vibrant, living city, caused by the absorption of noise by the plantings in the squares. The history of the city has unfolded in the squares. From the reading of the Declaration of Independence in 1776 to the passing of the Olympic torch in 1996, the squares are the city's heart. It is impossible to imagine life in Savannah without them.*

*Monterey Square is still considered by many to be the most beautiful square. All the elegant buildings around the square are original except one; among these princely dwellings are the famous Mercer House, the Charles Rogers double house with its exquisite lacy ironwork, the Cruger House where iron pelicans guard the steps, Comer House, which once hosted Jefferson Davis, and the Hardee mansion, a detail of which is illustrated here.*

# Sweets

Late Afternoon Sun  *by Laura Anne Ramberg*
*Illustration Undergraduate Student, The Savannah College of Art and Design*

# Banana Pound Cake

Beat the butter in a bowl at medium speed for 2 minutes or until creamy. Add the sugar gradually. Beat for 5 to 7 minutes longer or until blended, scraping the bowl occasionally. Add the eggs 1 at a time, beating well after each addition. Combine the bananas, milk and vanilla in a bowl and mix well. Combine the flour, baking powder and salt in a bowl and mix well. Add the flour mixture to the butter mixture alternately with the banana mixture, beating well at low speed after each addition. Spoon into a greased and floured 10-inch tube pan. Bake at 350 degrees for 1 hour. Cool in pan for 10 minutes. Remove to a serving platter. Yield: 12 servings.

1¹/₂ cups butter, softened
3 cups sugar
5 eggs
3 ripe bananas
3 tablespoons milk
1 teaspoon vanilla extract
3 cups flour
1 teaspoon baking powder
¹/₂ teaspoon salt

# Carrot Cake

*An old favorite—moist and yummy!*

Line the bottom of two 9-inch cake pans with waxed paper. Grease the sides of the pans and the waxed paper. Beat the sugar, oil and eggs in a mixer bowl until creamy. Add a sifted mixture of the flour, cinnamon, baking soda and salt and mix well. Stir in the vanilla. Fold in the carrots. Spoon into the prepared pans. Bake at 325 degrees for 35 to 45 minutes or until the layers test done. Cool in pans for 10 minutes. Remove to a wire rack to cool completely. For the frosting, beat the confectioners' sugar, cream cheese and butter in a mixer bowl until of spreading consistency. Stir in the pecans. Spread between the layers and over the top and side of the cake. Yield: 16 servings.

2 cups sugar
1¹/₂ cups vegetable oil
4 eggs
2 cups flour
1 tablespoon cinnamon
2 teaspoons baking soda
1 teaspoon salt
2 teaspoons vanilla extract
3 cups grated carrots

**Frosting**
1 (1-pound) package confectioners' sugar, sifted
8 ounces cream cheese, softened
¹/₂ cup melted butter
1 cup chopped pecans

# Chocolate Rum Cake

1   cup sugar
1/2   cup butter, softened
4   eggs, lightly beaten
1   (16-ounce) can chocolate syrup
1   cup flour
2   tablespoons rum

**Glaze**

1/2   cup semisweet chocolate chips
1/4   cup confectioners' sugar
2   tablespoons butter
2   tablespoons water
2   tablespoons rum
    Dash of salt

Cream the sugar and 1/2 cup butter in a bowl. Add the eggs. Beat at low speed until blended. Add the chocolate syrup, flour and 2 tablespoons rum. Beat at low speed until blended. Spoon into a greased 8-inch round cake pan. Bake at 350 degrees for 55 to 60 minutes or until the cake tests done. Cool in pan for 10 minutes. Remove to a wire rack to cool completely. Heat the chocolate chips, confectioners' sugar, 2 tablespoons butter, 2 tablespoons water, 2 tablespoons rum and salt in a saucepan until the chocolate chips melt, stirring constantly. Cool for 15 minutes. Spread over the cake. Yield: 8 servings.

# Fig Preserve Cake

2   cups flour
1 1/2   cups sugar
1   teaspoon each baking soda, salt, nutmeg and cinnamon
1/2   teaspoon ground cloves
1   cup vegetable oil
3   eggs
1   cup buttermilk
1   tablespoon vanilla extract
1   cup fig preserves, chopped
1/2   cup chopped pecans

**Glaze**

1/2   cup sugar
1/4   cup buttermilk
1 1/2   teaspoons cornstarch
1/4   teaspoon baking soda
1 1/2   teaspoons vanilla extract

Combine the flour, 1 1/2 cups sugar, 1 teaspoon baking soda, salt, nutmeg, cinnamon and cloves in a bowl and mix well. Add the oil. Beat until blended. Beat in the eggs. Add 1 cup buttermilk and 1 tablespoon vanilla and mix well. Stir in the preserves and pecans. Spoon into a greased and floured 10-inch tube pan. Bake at 350 degrees for 1 1/4 hours. Cool in pan for 10 minutes. Remove to a serving platter. *For the glaze*, bring 1/2 cup sugar, 1/4 cup buttermilk, cornstarch and 1/4 teaspoon baking soda to a boil in a saucepan. Remove from heat. Cool slightly. Stir in 1 1/2 teaspoons vanilla. Drizzle over the warm cake. May substitute dark purple figs or bronze figs for the fig preserves. Yield: 16 servings.

# Fresh Fruitcake

Beat $1/2$ cup sugar and $1/3$ cup butter in a bowl until creamy. Add the egg and vanilla, beating until blended. Add a mixture of the flour and baking powder alternately with the milk, mixing well after each addition. Spoon into a greased 7x11-inch cake pan. Arrange the apples in rows over the top. Dot with 2 tablespoons margarine. Sprinkle with 1 tablespoon sugar and cinnamon. Bake at 350 degrees for 30 to 35 minutes or until the edges pull from the sides of the pan. Serve with vanilla ice cream or whipped cream. May substitute 3 or 4 peaches, sliced, or 6 Italian plums, sliced, for the apples. Yield: 12 servings.

| | |
|---|---|
| $1/2$ | cup sugar |
| $1/3$ | cup butter or margarine, softened |
| 1 | egg |
| $1/2$ | teaspoon vanilla extract |
| 1 | cup flour |
| 1 | teaspoon baking powder |
| $1/2$ | cup milk |
| 2 | apples, peeled, sliced |
| 2 | tablespoons margarine or butter |
| 1 | tablespoon sugar |
| 1 | teaspoon cinnamon |

# Lemon Layer Cake

*Light and lemony flavor!*

Sift the cake flour, baking powder and salt together. Beat 1 cup butter in a bowl until creamy. Add 2 cups sugar gradually, beating constantly for 10 minutes. Beat in the eggs 1 at a time. Add the cake flour mixture alternately with the milk and both extracts, beating constantly. Spoon into 3 greased and floured cake pans. Bake at 350 degrees for 25 to 30 minutes or until the layers test done. Cool in pans for 10 minutes. Remove to wire racks to cool completely. *For the icing,* combine 2 cups sugar and all-purpose flour in a saucepan. Stir in the hot water, lemon juice, lemon peel and egg yolks. Cook until thickened, stirring constantly. Add $1/4$ cup butter and mix well. Cool slightly. Spread between the layers and over the top and side of the cake. Yield: 12 servings.

| | |
|---|---|
| 3 | cups sifted cake flour |
| 1 | tablespoon baking powder |
| $1^1/2$ | teaspoons salt |
| 1 | cup butter, softened |
| 2 | cups sugar |
| 4 | eggs |
| 1 | cup milk |
| $1^1/2$ | teaspoons almond extract |
| 1 | teaspoon vanilla extract |
| 2 | cups sugar |
| 6 | tablespoons all-purpose flour |
| 2 | cups hot water |
| | Juice and grated peel of 4 lemons |
| 4 | egg yolks |
| $1/4$ | cup butter |

# Light Pound Cake

3    cups cake flour
1    teaspoon baking powder
1    teaspoon salt
1/2  cup low-fat milk
1    teaspoon vanilla extract
3    cups (scant) sugar
1    cup butter, softened
1/2  cup shortening
5    eggs

Sift the cake flour, baking powder and salt together. Combine the low-fat milk and vanilla in a bowl and mix well. Beat the sugar, butter and shortening in a mixer bowl until creamy. Add the eggs 1 at a time, beating well after each addition. Add the flour mixture alternately with the milk mixture, beating at low speed just until blended. Fold the batter with a spatula to insure that all dry ingredients are incorporated into the batter. Spoon into a greased and floured tube pan; tap the pan to remove air bubbles. Bake at 325 degrees for 1 hour. Turn off the oven. Let stand with the door closed for 10 minutes. Cool on a wire rack for 10 minutes. Remove the cake from the pan with the tube and place on a cake plate. Let stand until cool. Remove the tube and slice just before serving. Yield: 16 servings.

# Peach Pound Cake

3    cups flour
3/4  teaspoon salt
1/4  teaspoon baking soda
2    cups chopped peeled peaches
1/2  cup sour cream
3    cups sugar
1    cup butter or margarine,
     softened
6    eggs
1    teaspoon vanilla extract
1    teaspoon almond extract

*A Georgia treat . . . a recipe to be made repeatedly.*

Mix the flour, salt and baking soda in a bowl. Combine the peaches and sour cream in a bowl and mix well. Cream the sugar and butter in a mixer bowl until light and fluffy, scraping the bowl occasionally. Add the eggs 1 at a time, beating well after each addition. Add the dry ingredients alternately with the peach mixture, beginning and ending with the dry ingredients and beating well after each addition. Stir in the vanilla and almond extracts. Spoon into a greased and floured 10-inch tube pan. Bake at 350 degrees for 75 to 80 minutes or until the cake tests done. Yield: 16 servings.

# Picnic Cupcakes

Spray 1¹/₂ dozen paper-lined muffin cups with nonstick cooking spray. Combine ¹/₂ cup butter and unsweetened chocolate in a microwave-safe dish. Microwave for 1 to 2 minutes or until blended, stirring once or twice. Combine the sugar, eggs, 1 teaspoon vanilla and chocolate mixture in a bowl and mix well. Add the flour, stirring just until blended. Stir in the nuts. Spoon into the prepared muffins cups. Bake at 350 degrees for 12 minutes. *For the frosting*, combine the semisweet chocolate and ¹/₄ cup butter in a microwave-safe dish. Microwave until blended, stirring once or twice. Add the confectioners' sugar alternately with the milk, mixing well after each addition and stirring until of spreading consistency. Blend in vanilla to taste. Spread over the warm cupcakes. Yield: 1¹/₂ dozen cupcakes.

¹/₂   *cup butter*
1¹/₂ *ounces unsweetened chocolate*
1    *cup sugar*
2    *eggs, beaten*
1    *teaspoon vanilla extract*
²/₃   *cup flour*
¹/₂   *cup chopped nuts (optional)*

**Frosting**
2    *ounces semisweet chocolate*
¹/₄   *cup butter*
1    *(1-pound) package confectioners' sugar*
¹/₄   *cup milk*
     *Vanilla extract to taste*

# Benne Crescents

*A Southern delicacy!*

Spread the benne seeds on a baking sheet. Toast at 250 degrees for 1 hour or until golden brown. Beat the butter, sugar and brown sugar in a mixer bowl until creamy. Blend in the vanilla and salt. Stir in the flour and benne seeds and mix well. Roll the dough on a lightly floured surface; cut into strips 1¹/₂ inches long. Shape into crescents on an ungreased cookie sheet. Bake at 300 degrees for 35 minutes or until light brown. Cool slightly. Roll the warm crescents in confectioners' sugar. Yield: 75 crescents.

³/₄   *cup benne seeds*
¹/₂   *cup butter, softened*
¹/₄   *cup sugar*
¹/₄   *cup packed brown sugar*
1    *teaspoon vanilla extract*
1    *teaspoon salt*
2    *cups flour*
     *Confectioners' sugar*

# Chocolate Chip Spice Cookies

1   cup sugar
3/4  cup vegetable oil
1/4  cup molasses
1   egg, beaten
2   cups flour
2   teaspoons baking soda
1   teaspoon ginger
1   teaspoon cinnamon
1   teaspoon ground cloves
3/4  cup semisweet chocolate chips
1/4  cup confectioners' sugar

*Traditional spice cookies with the added flavor of chocolate gives these cookies a very distinctive flavor.*

Combine the sugar, oil, molasses and egg in a bowl and mix well. Combine the flour, baking soda, ginger, cinnamon and cloves in a bowl and mix well. Stir into the sugar mixture. Fold in the chocolate chips. Shape by teaspoonfuls into balls; roll in confectioners' sugar. Arrange on a lightly greased or parchment-lined cookie sheet. Flatten slightly. Bake at 350 degrees for 8 to 10 minutes or until golden brown. Remove to a wire rack to cool. Yield: 50 to 60 cookies.

# Chocolate Meringue Drops

2   egg whites
1/2  cup sugar
6   ounces semisweet chocolate, melted
1/2  teaspoon vanilla extract
1/2  teaspoon almond extract
1   cup chopped walnuts

*Nice with afternoon tea or coffee or as a light after-dinner dessert.*

Beat the egg whites in a mixer bowl until foamy. Add the sugar 1 tablespoon at a time, beating until stiff peaks form. Fold in the chocolate, both extracts and walnuts with a spatula. Drop by 2 tablespoonfuls onto a parchment-lined cookie sheet. Bake for 10 to 15 minutes or until the tops are dry; do not overbake. Cool on the cookie sheet. Yield: 1 to 1 1/2 dozen.

# Chocolate Truffles

*Rich delicious flavor!*

Combine the chocolate chips and whipping cream in a heavy saucepan. Cook over medium heat until blended, stirring constantly; increase heat to high. Bring to a boil, stirring constantly. Chill until the mixture is cool and stiff enough to handle. Shape into 1-inch balls. Roll in baking cocoa, chopped nuts, confectioners' sugar, cinnamon-sugar or the coating of your choice. Place each truffle in a miniature muffin cup. Store in the refrigerator. Yield: 4 dozen truffles.

1    pound semisweet chocolate chips
1¹/₂ cups whipping cream
     Baking cocoa, chopped nuts,
     confectioners' sugar or
     cinnamon-sugar

# German Chocolate Cookies

Combine the chocolate and butter in a double boiler. Heat over hot water until blended, stirring frequently. Let stand until cool. Beat the eggs in a bowl until foamy. Add the sugar 2 tablespoons at a time, beating until thickened. Stir in the chocolate mixture, flour, baking powder, cinnamon and salt. Add the pecans and vanilla and mix well. Drop by teaspoonfuls onto a greased cookie sheet. Bake at 350 degrees for 8 to 10 minutes. Remove to a wire rack to cool. Yield: 3 dozen cookies.

8    ounces German's sweet
     chocolate
1    tablespoon butter
2    eggs
³/₄  cup sugar
¹/₄  cup flour
¹/₄  teaspoon baking powder
¹/₄  teaspoon cinnamon
¹/₈  teaspoon salt
³/₄  cup chopped pecans or walnuts
¹/₂  teaspoon vanilla extract

# Macaroon Meringues

3    *egg whites*
1    *cup (scant) sugar*
14  *saltine crackers, crushed*
1    *teaspoon almond or vanilla*
      *extract*
1    *cup chopped nuts*

*Can be prepared in advance and stored in an airtight container. Top with sherbet or fresh fruit.*

Beat the egg whites in a mixer bowl until foamy. Add the sugar gradually, beating until stiff peaks form. Fold in the crackers, flavoring and nuts. Drop by rounded tablespoonfuls onto a greased cookie sheet. Make indention in center of each meringue with a spoon. Bake at 300 degrees for 30 minutes. Cool on cookie sheet.
Yield: 6 to 8 servings.

# Oatmeal Lace Cookies

1½  *cups unsalted butter*
2    *eggs, lightly beaten*
3    *cups rolled oats*
1¾  *cups sugar*
1½  *tablespoons flour*
2    *teaspoons vanilla extract*
1    *teaspoon salt*

Heat the butter in a large saucepan over low heat until melted. Cool slightly. Stir in the eggs. Add the oats, sugar, flour, vanilla and salt and mix well. Drop by 1½ tablespoonfuls 3 inches apart onto a parchment-lined cookie sheet; flatten with a spoon. Bake at 325 degrees for 13 to 15 minutes or until golden brown. Remove to a wire rack to cool.
Yield: 25 cookies.

# Apple Bars

For the crust, combine the flour, butter, 2/3 cup sugar and 1/2 teaspoon vanilla in a bowl and mix well. Pat into the bottom of a 9x13-inch baking pan. Bake at 350 degrees for 10 minutes. Cool slightly. Increase the oven temperature to 450 degrees. For the filling, beat the cream cheese, 2 cups sugar, eggs and 2 teaspoons vanilla in a bowl until blended. Spread over the baked layer. For the topping, combine the apples, 2/3 cup sugar and cinnamon in a bowl and mix well. Spread over the prepared layers. Bake for 10 minutes. Reduce the oven temperature to 400 degrees. Bake for 20 minutes. Sprinkle with the almonds. Bake for 5 minutes longer. Let stand until cool. For the glaze, heat the preserves in a saucepan over low heat until of a spreading consistency, stirring occasionally. Spread over the baked layers. Freeze just until set. Cut into bars. Yield: 3 dozen bars.

**Crust**
2    cups flour
1    cup butter, softened
2/3  cup sugar
1/2  teaspoon vanilla extract

**Filling**
16   ounces cream cheese, softened
2    cups sugar
2    eggs, lightly beaten
2    teaspoons vanilla extract

**Topping**
4    cups thinly sliced apples
2/3  cup sugar
1    teaspoon cinnamon
1    cup slivered almonds

**Glaze**
1    (18-ounce) jar peach or apricot
     preserves

# White Chocolate Macadamia Bars

| | |
|---|---|
| 1 | cup packed brown sugar |
| 1/2 | cup butter, softened |
| 1/2 | cup sugar |
| 2 | eggs |
| 1 1/2 | teaspoons vanilla extract |
| 2 | cups flour |
| 1 | teaspoon baking soda |
| 1 | teaspoon salt |
| 1 | cup chopped macadamia nuts |
| 2 | cups white chocolate chips |

Beat the brown sugar, butter and sugar in a mixer bowl until creamy. Add the eggs and vanilla and mix well. Blend in a mixture of the flour, baking soda and salt. Stir in the macadamia nuts and white chocolate chips. Spread into a greased 9x13-inch baking pan. Bake at 350 degrees for 30 to 35 minutes or until the edges pull from the sides of the pan. Let stand until cool. Cut into bars.
Yield: 30 bars.

# The Best Brownies

| | |
|---|---|
| 3/4 | cup packed brown sugar |
| 1/2 | cup unsalted butter, softened |
| 1 | teaspoon vanilla extract |
| 1/4 | teaspoon salt |
| 2 | eggs |
| 3/4 | cup Ghirardelli ground chocolate |
| 1/2 | cup flour |
| 1/2 | cup chocolate chips |
| 1/2 | cup white chocolate chips |
| 1/2 | cup chopped pecans (optional) |

*The world's most incredible brownie. Enjoy!*

Beat the brown sugar, butter, vanilla and salt in a bowl until creamy. Add the eggs 1 at a time. Add the chocolate, stirring just until blended. Stir in the flour, chocolate chips, white chocolate chips and pecans. Spoon into an 8x8-inch baking pan. Bake at 350 degrees for 25 to 35 minutes or until the edges pull from the sides of the pan. Cool in the pan on a wire rack. Cut into squares.
Yield: 20 brownies.

# Cream Cheese Squares

Combine the flour, brown sugar, butter and pecans in a bowl and mix well. Pat over the bottom of an 8x12-inch baking dish sprayed with nonstick cooking spray. Bake at 375 degrees for 10 to 15 minutes or until brown. Combine the cream cheese, 1 cup sugar, eggs and 1 teaspoon vanilla in a bowl. Beat until blended, scraping the bowl occasionally. Spread over the baked layer. Bake for 20 minutes longer. Cool in the pan on a wire rack. Combine the sour cream, 1/3 cup sugar and 1 teaspoon vanilla in a bowl and mix well. Spread over the baked layers. Bake at 375 degrees for 3 to 5 minutes. Let stand until cool. Chill for several hours. Cut into squares with a moistened knife. Garnish with sliced kiwi and sliced strawberries. May be frozen for future use.
Yield: 2 dozen squares.

**Crust**
1    cup flour
1/4  cup packed brown sugar
1/2  cup butter, softened
1    cup pecans, crushed

16   ounces cream cheese, softened
1    cup sugar
3    eggs
1    teaspoon vanilla extract
2    cups sour cream
1/3  cup sugar
1    teaspoon vanilla extract
     *Kiwi (optional)*
     *Strawberries (optional)*

# Chilled Blueberry Pie

4  cups fresh blueberries
2  tablespoons cornstarch
2  tablespoons water
1/2  cup light corn syrup
2  teaspoons lemon juice
1  cup whipping cream
2  tablespoons confectioners' sugar
1  (9-inch) cinnamon graham cracker pie shell
1  lemon, sliced (optional)

*A blue ribbon pie that is at its best made with plump, fresh blueberries.*

Process 1 cup of the blueberries in a blender or food processor until puréed. Combine the cornstarch and water in a saucepan and mix well. Stir in the blueberry purée, corn syrup and lemon juice. Bring to a boil. Boil for 1 minute, stirring constantly. Cool for 1 hour. Fold in the remaining 3 cups blueberries. Beat the whipping cream in a mixer bowl until foamy. Add the confectioners' sugar gradually, beating constantly until stiff peaks form. Spread over the bottom and side of the pie shell, forming a 1-inch shell. Spoon the blueberry mixture into the prepared pie shell. Chill for 4 hours. Garnish with lemon slices. Yield: 6 servings.

# Chocolate Ice Cream-Peanut Butter Pie

22  chocolate sandwich cookies
1/4  cup melted unsalted butter
3  cups vanilla ice cream, softened
1/2  cup peanut butter
3  cups chocolate ice cream, softened
1  cup semisweet chocolate chips
1/4  cup milk, scalded
3  tablespoons coarsely chopped peanuts

*Decadence at its best! Thin slices are recommended because it is very rich.*

Process the cookies in a food processor until crushed. Mix with the butter in a bowl. Press over the bottom and up the side of an ungreased 9-inch pie plate. Freeze for several hours or overnight. Spoon the vanilla ice cream into the prepared pie shell. Freeze for 45 minutes. Spread the peanut butter evenly over the ice cream. Freeze for 20 minutes. Spoon the chocolate ice cream over the prepared layers. Freeze for 2 hours or until firm. Mix the chocolate chips and milk in a bowl. Let stand until cool. Spread over the prepared layers. Sprinkle with the peanuts. Freeze until serving time. Yield: 8 to 10 servings.

# Fudge Pie

*Fudge at its finest!*

Combine the butter and chocolate in a double boiler. Cook over low heat until blended, stirring frequently. Cool slightly. Beat the eggs in a mixer bowl until pale yellow. Add the sugar, corn syrup, vanilla and salt, beating until blended. Stir in the chocolate mixture. Spoon into the pie shell. Bake at 350 degrees for 35 to 45 minutes or until set and the top is crusty; pie should shake like custard. Do not overbake. Let stand until cool. Serve with vanilla ice cream or whipped cream. Yield: 6 to 8 servings.

| | |
|---|---|
| $^1/_2$ | cup butter |
| 3 | ounces unsweetened chocolate |
| 4 | eggs |
| $1^1/_2$ | cups sugar |
| 3 | tablespoons light corn syrup |
| 1 | teaspoon vanilla extract |
| $^1/_4$ | teaspoon salt |
| 1 | unbaked (9-inch) pie shell |

# Perfect Peach Pie

*Perfect!*

Combine the flour, butter and confectioners' sugar in a bowl, mixing until a soft dough forms. Pat over the bottom and up the side of a 9-inch metal pie plate. Bake at 350 degrees for 20 minutes or until light brown. Bring 1 cup sugar, water, cornstarch, gelatin and salt to a rolling boil in a saucepan, stirring occasionally. Remove from heat. Let stand until cool. Add a mixture of the peaches, 1 tablespoon sugar and lemon juice and mix gently. Spoon into the baked pie shell. Spread with the whipped cream, sealing to the edge. Chill until serving time. Do not substitute margarine for the butter in this recipe. Yield: 6 to 8 servings.

| | |
|---|---|
| 1 | cup flour |
| $^1/_2$ | cup butter, softened |
| $^1/_4$ | cup confectioners' sugar |
| 1 | cup sugar |
| 1 | cup water |
| 3 | tablespoons cornstarch |
| $^1/_4$ | cup peach gelatin |
| | Pinch of salt |
| 2 | cups (heaping) chopped peaches |
| 1 | tablespoon sugar |
| $^1/_2$ | teaspoon lemon juice |
| 1 | cup whipping cream, whipped |

# Pecan Almond Tart

## Crust

| | |
|---|---|
| 1/2 | cup unbleached flour |
| 1/4 | cup whole wheat pastry flour |
| 1/4 | cup unsalted butter, chilled, cubed |
| 1 | tablespoon sugar |
| 1/2 | teaspoon nutmeg |
| 2 | tablespoons very cold water |

## Filling

| | |
|---|---|
| 3/4 | cup light corn syrup |
| 1/2 | cup sugar |
| 3 | tablespoons unsalted butter, chilled |
| 3 | eggs |
| 1 | teaspoon vanilla extract |
| 1 | cup chopped pecans, toasted |
| 1/3 | cup sliced almonds |

*This recipe was contributed by Elizabeth's on 37th.*

*For the crust*, butter a 9-inch tart pan. Process the unbleached flour, whole wheat flour, 1/4 cup butter, 1 tablespoon sugar and nutmeg in a food processor until crumbly. Add the cold water gradually, processing constantly for several seconds or until the mixture forms a ball. Shape the dough into a flat circle. Chill, wrapped in plastic wrap, for 30 minutes. Roll the dough into a 9-inch circle on a lightly floured surface. Fit into the prepared tart pan; prick with a fork. Be careful that there are no breaks in the crust. Chill for 30 minutes or longer. Line the prepared tart pan with foil; fill with 2 cups dried beans. Bake at 375 degrees for 10 minutes; remove the beans and foil. Bake for 5 minutes longer. Let stand until cool. *For the filling*, bring the corn syrup and 1/2 cup sugar to a boil in a saucepan. Boil for 2 minutes or until the sugar dissolves and is of a syrupy consistency, stirring frequently. Remove from heat. Stir in 3 tablespoons butter. Cool for 5 minutes. Whisk the eggs in a bowl until blended. Add the syrup and vanilla, whisking until blended. Strain into the prepared tart pan. Sprinkle with the pecans and almonds. Bake for 30 minutes. Let stand until cool. May substitute a 9-inch pie plate for the tart pan. Yield: 6 to 8 servings.

# Blueberry Cobbler

*Recipe easily doubled. If desired, serve warm with a scoop of vanilla ice cream or a dollop of whipped cream. Delicious and simple to prepare.*

Microwave the butter in a 1¹/₂-quart microwave-safe dish until melted. Combine the flour, sugar, baking powder and salt in a bowl and mix well. Add the skim milk gradually, stirring until blended. Pour into the prepared dish. Sprinkle with the blueberries. Bake at 350 degrees for 40 to 45 minutes or until bubbly. Yield: 8 servings.

2   tablespoons butter
²/₃  cup flour
¹/₂  cup sugar
1¹/₂ teaspoons baking powder
¹/₄  teaspoon salt
²/₃  cup skim milk
2   cups drained blueberries

# Almond Pudding

Combine the milk and butter in a saucepan. Heat until the butter melts and the mixture is warm. Beat the eggs in a bowl until blended. Add the sugar gradually, beating well after each addition. Add the milk mixture gradually and mix well. Stir in the bread crumbs and both extracts. Pour into a greased baking dish. Place in a pan larger than the baking dish. Add enough water to the pan to reach halfway up the sides of the baking dish. Bake at 275 degrees for 1 hour or longer. May sprinkle with nutmeg before baking or add 2 tablespoons cream sherry. Yield: 4 to 6 servings.

2¹/₂ cups milk
3   tablespoons butter
4   eggs
³/₄  cup plus 2 tablespoons sugar
2¹/₂ cups dry bread crumbs without crusts
2   teaspoons almond extract
2   teaspoons vanilla extract
     Nutmeg (optional)
2   tablespoons cream sherry (optional)

# Bread Pudding with Whiskey Sauce

<sup>1</sup>/<sub>2</sub>  cup raisins
4  cups milk
1<sup>1</sup>/<sub>2</sub>  cups sugar
1  cup whipping cream
4  eggs
<sup>1</sup>/<sub>2</sub>  cup chopped pecans
1  teaspoon cinnamon
1  teaspoon nutmeg
1  teaspoon vanilla extract
1  (14-ounce) loaf dry French
   bread
6  tablespoons butter
   Whiskey Sauce

Combine the raisins with enough warm water to cover in a bowl. Let stand for 2 hours; drain. Combine the milk, sugar, whipping cream and eggs in a bowl, whisking until mixed. Stir in the pecans and raisins. Add the cinnamon, nutmeg and vanilla and mix well. Break the bread into the milk mixture, mixing until the bread is moistened. Spoon into a buttered 9x13-inch baking dish. Dot with the butter. Place the baking dish in a pan larger than the baking dish; add water to the pan to a depth of <sup>1</sup>/<sub>2</sub> inch. Bake at 350 degrees for 30 minutes. Remove from the water bath. Bake for 45 minutes longer. Serve warm topped with Whiskey Sauce. Yield: 15 to 18 servings.

# Whiskey Sauce

3 eggs
1 cup sugar
1/2 cup milk
1 teaspoon vanilla extract
1/4 cup cold water
1 tablespoon cornstarch
3 tablespoons Canadian whiskey

Whisk the eggs in a double boiler over medium heat until slightly thickened. Stir in the sugar, milk and vanilla. Cook until heated through, stirring frequently; do not allow to boil. Stir in a mixture of the cold water and cornstarch. Add the whiskey and mix well. Cook over medium heat for 15 minutes or until thickened, stirring frequently. Serve chilled or at room temperature.
Yield: 15 to 18 servings.

# Russian Cream with Berries

Sprinkle the gelatin over the cold water in a saucepan. Let stand for 5 minutes. Simmer over low heat until the gelatin dissolves, stirring frequently. Combine the gelatin mixture with the boiling water in a bowl and mix well. Add the sugar, stirring until dissolved. Stir in the whipping cream and vanilla. Whisk the sour cream. Add to the gelatin mixture, mixing until blended. Spoon into a 1-quart mold or 6 individual parfait glasses. Chill until set. Invert the mold onto a serving platter. Garnish with fresh berries and mint sprigs. Serve with a mixture of the strawberries and raspberries. May substitute fresh fruit for the frozen fruit. Yield: 6 servings.

| | |
|---|---|
| 1 | envelope unflavored gelatin |
| 1/4 | cup cold water |
| 3/4 | cup boiling water |
| 3/4 | cup sugar |
| 1 | cup whipping cream |
| 1 | teaspoon vanilla extract |
| 1 | cup sour cream |
| 1 | (10-ounce) package frozen strawberries, thawed, drained |
| 1 | (10-ounce) package frozen raspberries, thawed, drained |
| | Fresh berries (optional) |
| | Mint leaves (optional) |

# Lemon Bisque

Chill the evaporated milk for 24 hours. Spread the vanilla wafer crumbs in the bottom of a springform pan sprayed with nonstick cooking spray. Combine the gelatin, sugar, salt, lemon juice, lemon peel and boiling water in a bowl and mix well. Set the bowl in a larger bowl of ice water. Let mixture stand until slightly thickened or of the consistency of egg whites. Beat the evaporated milk in a bowl until stiff peaks form. Fold into the gelatin mixture. Spoon into the prepared springform pan. Chill overnight. Yield: 6 to 8 servings.

| | |
|---|---|
| 1 | (12-ounce) can evaporated milk |
| 1/2 | cup vanilla wafer crumbs |
| 1 | (3-ounce) package lemon gelatin |
| 1/3 | cup sugar |
| 1/4 | teaspoon salt |
| 3 | tablespoons lemon juice |
| | Grated peel of 1 lemon |
| 1 1/2 | cups boiling water |

# Easy Cream Caramel

**Caramel**
1   cup sugar
¹/₃   cup water

**Custard**
3   eggs
2   egg yolks
6   tablespoons sugar
1   teaspoon vanilla extract
    Pinch of salt
2   cups milk, heated

*For the caramel*, combine 1 cup sugar and water in a 6- to 8-cup microwave-safe dish; cover tightly with plastic wrap. Microwave on High for 7 to 8 minutes; remove the plastic wrap. Microwave for 2 minutes longer or until the caramel is a rich brown. *For the custard*, beat the eggs, egg yolks, 6 tablespoons sugar, vanilla and salt in a bowl until mixed but not foamy. Add a small amount of the egg mixture to the hot milk; stir the hot milk into the egg mixture. Pour into the caramel-lined dish. Place the dish in a pan larger than the dish. Add water to a depth of 1 inch. Bake at 350 degrees for 45 minutes or until a knife inserted in the center comes out clean. Let cool. Chill for several hours. Dip the dish into hot water for 10 seconds. Invert onto a serving platter. The caramel will melt and run down the sides. Yield: 6 servings.

# Mocha Velvet Mousse

3   egg yolks
2   tablespoons crème de cacao
2   tablespoons rum
1   tablespoon instant coffee
    granules
1   pound semisweet chocolate
5   tablespoons plus 1 teaspoon
    butter
¹/₂   cup confectioners' sugar
4   cups whipping cream
3   egg whites, stiffly beaten
    Sugar to taste
    Semisweet chocolate shavings

Mix the egg yolks, crème de cacao, rum and coffee granules in a bowl. Heat the chocolate and butter in a double boiler over simmering water until blended, stirring frequently. Remove from heat. Stir in the confectioners' sugar. Let cool. Stir into the egg yolk mixture. Beat 2 cups of the whipping cream in a bowl until stiff peaks form. Fold in the egg whites. Fold into the chocolate mixture. Spoon into a serving bowl or individual dessert dishes. Chill until set or overnight. Beat the remaining 2 cups whipping cream in a bowl until soft peaks form. Add the desired amount of sugar and mix well. Top each serving with whipped cream and sprinkle with chocolate shavings.
Yield: 10 to 12 servings.

# Margarita Cheesecake

Combine the pretzel crumbs and butter in a bowl and mix well. Press over the bottom and 2 inches up the side of a 9-inch springform pan. Bake at 325 degrees for 8 to 10 minutes or until brown. Beat the cream cheese in a mixer bowl at medium speed until fluffy, scraping the bowl occasionally. Add the sugar gradually, beating well after each addition. Add the eggs 1 at a time, beating well after each addition. Stir in the lime juice, tequila and Triple Sec. Spoon into the prepared pan. Spread the strawberry purée in a circle over the prepared layers. Pull a knife gently through the purée to the side to make a spoke pattern. Bake at 325 degrees for 1 hour and 10 minutes. Remove from oven. Turn off the oven. Loosen the cheesecake from the side of the pan with a sharp knife. Return the cheesecake to the oven. Let stand for 30 minutes and then remove. Transfer to a wire rack to cool completely. Remove the side of the pan. Chill, covered with plastic wrap, for 8 hours. (Do not cover with foil.) Garnish with thinly sliced limes and strawberries just before serving. Yield: 12 servings.

**Crust**

1³/₄ cups pretzel crumbs
³/₄ cup melted butter

**Filling**

24 ounces cream cheese, softened
1 cup sugar
4 eggs
¹/₄ cup freshly squeezed lime juice
¹/₄ cup tequila
¹/₄ cup Triple Sec
¹/₂ cup strawberry purée
1 lime, thinly sliced (optional)
 Sliced strawberries (optional)

# Summer Shortcake

2 cups flour, sifted
1 tablespoon baking powder
3/4 teaspoon salt
1/2 cup butter or margarine,
   softened
1/4 cup packed light brown sugar
1/2 cup (about) milk

**Fruit Filling**
4 cups sliced strawberries and/or
   peaches
1/4 to 1/2 cup packed light brown
   sugar
   Lemon juice to taste

**Cream**
1 cup whipping cream
1 teaspoon confectioners' sugar
1 teaspoon vanilla extract

*A must when summer fruits are at their peak. In the winter, equally good with frozen fruits.*

Combine the flour, baking powder and salt in a bowl and mix well. Cut in the butter and 1/4 cup brown sugar with a pastry blender. Make a well in the center of the mixture. Pour the milk into the well. Mix with a pastry blender until the dough forms a ball; do not over mix. Knead on a lightly floured surface 10 times. Pat the dough into a greased 8-inch round cake pan. Bake at 425 degrees for 20 minutes or until brown. *For the filling,* combine the strawberries, 1/4 to 1/2 cup brown sugar and lemon juice in a bowl and mix gently. Let stand. Beat the whipping cream in a mixer bowl untilsoft peaks form. Add the confectioners' sugarand vanilla and mix well. Split the shortcake horizontally. Place the bottom half on a serving platter. Arrange 1/2 of the strawberries over the shortcake half; spread with a thin layer of the whipped cream. Top with the remaining shortcake half, remaining strawberries and remaining whipped cream. Garnish with whole strawberries. Yield: 8 to 10 servings.

# Toffee Trifle

*A new twist for trifle. Grind the toffee at the last possible minute!*

Prepare the pudding mix using package directions, substituting half-and-half for the milk. Drizzle the Kahlúa over the angel food cake in a bowl. Let stand for 5 minutes. Fold in the pudding. Mix the whipping cream and coffee granules in a bowl. Let stand for 1 minute. Beat until soft peaks form. Add the sugar and vanilla; beat until stiff peaks form. Reserve 1¹/₂ cups of the whipped cream. Layer the cake mixture, remaining whipped cream and toffee ¹/₂ at a time in a 2-quart serving bowl. Pipe the reserved whipped cream around the edge of the bowl. Chill until serving time. Yield: 10 to 12 servings.

1   (6-ounce) package vanilla instant pudding mix
3   cups half-and-half
³/₄  cup Kahlúa
1   (1-pound) angel food cake, cut into 1¹/₂-inch cubes
2   cups whipping cream
2   tablespoons instant coffee granules
2   tablespoons sugar
1   teaspoon vanilla extract
8   ounces English toffee, coarsely crushed

# Peanut Butter and Chocolate Treasures

For the crust, combine the flour, brown sugar, baking powder, baking soda and salt in a bowl and mix well. Add the ²/₃ cup butter, egg yolks and ¹/₂ teaspoon vanilla. Beat at low speed until crumbly. Pat into an ungreased 9x13-inch baking pan. Bake at 350 degrees for 12 minutes. Remove from oven. Turn off the oven. Let crust stand for 2 minutes. *For the filling*, combine the peanut butter, confectioners' sugar, ¹/₄ cup butter and ¹/₂ teaspoon vanilla in a bowl and mix well. Spread over the baked layer. Sprinkle with the chocolate chips. Place in the warm oven for 3 minutes or until the chocolate chips soften. Spread the chocolate chips evenly over the top. Let stand until cool. Cut into bars. Yield: 36 bars.

**Crust**
1¹/₂ cups flour
²/₃  cup packed brown sugar
¹/₂  teaspoon baking powder
¹/₄  teaspoon baking soda
¹/₈  teaspoon salt
²/₃  cup butter, softened
2   egg yolks, beaten
¹/₂  teaspoon vanilla extract

**Filling**
1¹/₂ cups crunchy peanut butter
1¹/₄ cups confectioners' sugar
¹/₄  cup melted butter
¹/₂  teaspoon vanilla extract
2   cups semisweet chocolate chips

# Pumpkin Roll

3/4  cup flour
2    teaspoons cinnamon
1    teaspoon baking powder
1    teaspoon ginger
1/2  teaspoon salt
1/2  teaspoon nutmeg
3    eggs
1    cup sugar
2/3  cup canned pumpkin
1    teaspoon lemon juice
1    cup finely chopped pecans

## Filling
1    cup confectioners' sugar
6    ounces cream cheese, softened
1/4  cup butter, softened
1/2  teaspoon vanilla extract

Grease a large jelly roll pan; line with waxed paper. Grease and flour the waxed paper. Combine the flour, cinnamon, baking powder, ginger, salt and nutmeg in a bowl and mix well. Beat the eggs in a bowl at high speed for 5 minutes. Add the sugar gradually, beating constantly until blended. Stir in the pumpkin and lemon juice. Fold in the dry ingredients. Spread in the prepared pan. Sprinkle with the pecans. Bake at 375 degrees for 15 minutes. Invert onto a tea towel sprinkled with additional confectioners' sugar. Let stand until cool. Beat 1 cup confectioners' sugar, cream cheese, butter and vanilla in a mixer bowl until smooth, scraping the bowl occasionally. Spread over the baked layer; roll as for a jelly roll. Chill until serving time. Slice just before serving. Yield: 12 to 15 servings.

# Chocolate Chambord Pâté with Gingered Pear Sorbet

*This recipe was contributed by 45 South.*

Combine the chocolate, butter, Chambord and water in a double boiler. Heat over simmering water until blended, stirring frequently. Remove from heat. Cool slightly. Whisk in the egg yolks. Strain into a mold. Chill until set. Serve with Pear Sorbet. For health purposes, pasteurized egg product may be used in place of egg yolks. Yield: 4 servings.

| | |
|---|---|
| 1 | pound bittersweet chocolate, chopped |
| 3/4 | cup unsalted butter, cubed |
| 1/4 | cup Chambord |
| 1/2 | cup water |
| 2 | egg yolks, beaten, or equivalent pasteurized egg product |
| | Pear Sorbet |

## Pear Sorbet

Combine the pears, sugar and white wine in a saucepan. Simmer until the pears are tender, stirring frequently. Stir in the ginger. Remove from heat. Let stand until cool. Discard the ginger. Process pear mixture in a blender until puréed. Pour into an ice cream freezer container. Freeze using manufacturers' directions. Yield: 4 servings.

| | |
|---|---|
| 14 | ounces pears, peeled, chopped |
| 1/2 | cup plus 2 tablespoons sugar |
| 1/2 | cup plus 2 tablespoons white wine |
| 1 | small piece ginger |

# Layered Fruits in Lemon Pear Sauce with Toasted Almonds

1   (29-ounce) can pear halves in heavy syrup
2   tablespoons flour
1   egg, beaten
2   teaspoons lemon juice
1   teaspoon butter
1   cup whipping cream
2   tablespoons confectioners' sugar
2   cups coarsely chopped fresh pineapple
1   medium banana, sliced
1   pint strawberries, sliced
1   (11-ounce) can mandarin oranges, drained
2   kiwi, chilled, peeled, sliced
1/4 cup slivered almonds, toasted

Drain the pears, reserving 1 cup of the syrup. Cut 4 of the pear halves lengthwise into halves and reserve. Chop the remaining pears. Combine the reserved pear syrup, flour and egg in a saucepan and mix well. Cook over medium heat until thickened, stirring constantly. Stir in the lemon juice and butter. Let stand until cool. Beat the whipping cream in a bowl until soft peaks form. Add the confectioners' sugar and beat until stiff peaks form. Fold into the syrup mixture. Layer the chopped pears, pineapple, banana, strawberries and mandarin oranges in a glass serving bowl. Spread with the whipped cream mixture. Chill, covered, overnight. Top with the reserved pear slices, kiwi and almonds just before serving. Yield: 8 to 10 servings.

# Red Wine Poached Pears

6   firm small Bosc or Bartlett pears
    Juice of 1 lemon
3   cups dry red wine
1   cup sugar
1/2 cup water
    Juice of 1 orange
2   teaspoons grated lemon zest
2   teaspoons grated orange zest
1   star anise
3   whole cloves
2   cinnamon sticks

Peel the pears; remove the cores from the bottom. Place the pears in a bowl. Combine the lemon juice with enough cold water to cover the pears in the bowl. Pour over the pears. Combine the red wine, sugar, 1/2 cup water, orange juice, lemon zest, orange zest, star anise, cloves and cinnamon sticks in a saucepan. Bring to a boil. Add the pears; reduce heat to low. Poach for 35 minutes or until tender. Transfer the pears to a bowl with a slotted spoon. Let the poaching liquid stand until cool. Pour over the pears. Chill, covered, for 8 to 48 hours. Discard the star anise, cloves and cinnamon sticks. Serve at room temperature or reheat until warm. Serve with a slice of Brie cheese or Camembert cheese. Yield: 6 servings.

# Index

# Order Information

*Please send me:*

____ copies of *Savannah Style*  @ $18.95 each  $ _____
Georgia residents add $1.14 sales tax each  $ _____

____ copies of *Downtown Savannah Style*  @ $14.95 each  $ _____
Georgia residents add $0.90 sales tax each  $ _____

Add postage and handling @ $ 2.50 each  $ _____
Subtract $1.00 on orders of two or more books  $ _____

Total Enclosed  $ _____

Name _____

Address _____

City/State/Zip _____

Telephone _____

*Make checks payable to:*  Junior League of Savannah
P.O. Box 1864 · Savannah, Georgia 31402
www.jrleaguesav.org

---

*Please send me:*

____ copies of *Savannah Style*  @ $18.95 each  $ _____
Georgia residents add $1.14 sales tax each  $ _____

____ copies of *Downtown Savannah Style*  @ $14.95 each  $ _____
Georgia residents add $0.90 sales tax each  $ _____

Add postage and handling @ $ 2.50 each  $ _____
Subtract $1.00 on orders of two or more books  $ _____

Total Enclosed  $ _____

Name _____

Address _____

City/State/Zip _____

Telephone _____

*Make checks payable to:*  Junior League of Savannah
P.O. Box 1864 · Savannah, Georgia 31402
www.jrleaguesav.org

All profits from cookbook sales are returned to the community through the Junior League of Savannah.